Code of Practice for Community Equipment

A C   and

Published by Community Equipment Solutions Ltd.

105879

Published and distributed by:
Community Equipment Solutions Ltd.
Aston Court
Kingsmead Business Park
High Wycombe
Buckinghamshire
HP11 1LA
E: info@communityequipment.org.uk
W: www.communityequipment.org.uk

British Library Cataloguing in Publication Data. A catalogue record for this book is available from the British Library.

Printed and bound in the UK.

ISBN number 978-0-9569095-0-3

Contents

Forewords   vii
Preface   xi
Acknowledgements   xv
About the Community Equipment Code of Practice Scheme   xvii

Introduction   1

Part 1: Commissioning and Governance   3

Code standard 1 - Service Requirements and Specifications   6

Code standard 2 - Partnerships, Joint Working and Pooled Funding   7

Code standard 3 - Funding Arrangements   10

Code standard 4 - Contractual Arrangements   12

Code standard 5 - Legal and Welfare Obligations   13

Code standard 6 - Governance and Risk Management   15

Code standard 7 - Eligibility Criteria   18

Code standard 8 - Contract and Performance Management   20

Part 2: Service Provision   25

Code standard 9   - Operational Management   26

Code standard 10 - Quality Management Systems   28

Code standard 11 - Training and Qualifications   30

Code standard 12 - Information Technology and Information Management 32

Code standard 13 - Health and Safety Management   34

Code standard 14 - Transportation   37

Code standard 15 - Decontamination   39

Code standard 16 - Performance Management   42

Code standard 17 - Emergency and Out of Hour Cover   43

Code standard 18 - Stock Management   45

Code standard 19 - Recycling   46

Code standard 20 - Assembling, Fitting and Demonstrating Equipment   47

Code standard 21 - Minor Adaptations   49

Code standard 22 - Manual Handling   51

Code standard 23 - Medical Device Management   52

Part 3: Clinical and Professional Responsibilities   55

Code standard 24 - Assessing the Service User's Equipment Needs   57

Code standard 25 - Single Assessment (Co-ordinated Approach)   59

Code standard 26 - Assessing the Home   60

Code standard 27 - Training in Equipment Provision and Use   61

Code standard 28 - Transportation of Equipment   63

Code standard 29 - Equipment Selection Process (New Acquisitions)   64

Code standard 30 - Demonstrating and Trialling Complex, Specialist and   67
Children's Equipment

Code standard 31 - Community Equipment Related Risk Assessments   69

Code standard 32 - Reviewing Equipment and Equipment Needs   71

Code standard 33 - Trusted Assessor   73

Code standard 34 - Self-Assessment   74

Code standard 35 - Financial and Budgetary Authorisation Processes   75

Part 4: Peripheral Issues and Specialist Areas   77

Code standard 36 - Community Equipment in Special Schools   77

Code standard 37 - Complex, Specialist and Children's Equipment   79

Code standard 38 - Continuing Healthcare Equipment   81

Code standard 39 - Community Equipment in Care Homes   83

Code standard 40 - Hospital Discharge Arrangements   84

Code standard 41 - Direct Payments   86

Code standard 42 - Links to Related Services, e.g. Wheelchairs, Telecare   88

Code standard 43 - Third Party Contractors   90

Code standard 44 - Outsourced Service Providers   91

Code standard 45 - Involvement of Users and Carers   92

Code standard 46 - Cross Border Protocol   93

Code standard 47 - Disabled Facilities Grants (DFGs) and Major Adaptations   95

Appendices   **99**

Appendix 1   101
The legal and welfare framework relating to community equipment

Appendix 2   125
Guide for contract management indicators

Appendix 3   129
SEMTA Occupational Standards specifically for community equipment
technicians

Appendix 4   131
Supporting guidance relating to training on Information Systems and
Information Management for individual roles

Appendix 5   133
Supporting guidance relating to Medical Device Management

Appendix 6   143
Health and Safety Executive (HSE) 'POPMAR' Model

Appendix 7   145
Supporting guidance relating to the choice of decontamination method
appropriate to the degree of infection risk associated with the intended
use of the equipment

Appendix 8   147
Glossary

Forewords

"I very much welcome this Code of Practice for a number of reasons. The first is that I have been disabled for almost all of my life and I know the vital role equipment has played in my life. Without disability equipment many of the things I have achieved in life would have been impossible. Professor Heinz Wolff defined disability equipment as "tools for living" and he was right to do so. We need the right tools at the right time. This Code should be a great help in enabling the providers of equipment to ensure their services are sensitive to the needs of users.

One of the peculiarities of equipment services in Britain is that different agencies are responsible for providing different types of equipment depending on the purpose for which the equipment is required. One of the claimed advantages of the proposed changes to the NHS is that it will unify services. This is an objective that has been sought for decades and it is possible to do no more than speculate whether future changes will be more successful than those of the past. But there will be upheaval and at such time the potential for errors increases. The Code recommends detailed procedures which, if followed, will help ensure that changes do not have a negative impact on service users.

The funding available to each user of the NHS is to be cut. Demand will increase while budgets remain at best static. This means that either service will be reduced or ways must be found to maintain services with reduced funding. How can costs be reduced without diminishing service? This Code provides ways of measuring the service and its performance. It is particularly welcome that it has been compiled with the support of the industry and is more likely to be implemented as a consequence.

It seems to me that there is a danger hard pressed officials will seek to amend services so they can balance the books. My view is that the best way to balance the books is to involve the users of the service. Disabled people are not fools and nor should we be passive recipients of services provided by professionals. I therefore welcome the parts of the Code that refer to user involvement. For many of us disability is not an event but a long term feature of our lives. We know that a short term solution can often have long term consequences that cost more to manage than could ever be saved by the cost conscious short term solution. This Code looks long term and that must be right.

The right equipment at the right time should be seen as an investment rather than expenditure. Impairments can be prevented from deteriorating, and accidents can be prevented, by the appropriate use of equipment. It is of course essential that users are trained to use the equipment, and the Code refers to this.

One of the consequences of the proposed changes to the NHS is that GP consortia will be responsible for commissioning services. This will include equipment. Whatever the qualities of GPs, few would regard themselves as expert in disability equipment. This Code will be a valuable guide for them as they assume their new responsibilities. If they fail to give a good service the result will be increased ill health and disability for their patients at an increased cost to their budgets. Health and Wellbeing Boards will also find the Code a helpful starting point, in commissioning services across the sectors.

There are different views about the retail model of provision. What is clear is that the various models all require highly skilled assessments to ensure disabled people receive the most appropriate equipment. The Code stresses this and the fact that commercial providers need to have many of the skills that were once the preserve of health professionals.

Brian Donnelly has spent many years seeking ways of improving the equipment service that disabled people receive. In writing this Code of Practice he has sought to provide a template for a service of the future that can withstand the short term pressures of today. I very much welcome it and hope that it is a Code that will be used and followed. It should find a place not just in the offices of the main service providers but also in special schools and residential accommodation: in fact, everywhere where disabled people use equipment."

Sir Bert Massie CBE

Sir Bert Massie CBE was the Commissioner for the Compact from 2008-2011. He has spent most of his adult life promoting equality and human rights of disabled people. From 2000-2007 he was Chairman of the Disability Rights Commission. Prior to that he was the chief executive of The Royal Association for Disability and Rehabilitation (RADAR) and was instrumental in ensuring that parliament passed the Disability Discrimination Act 1995. He has close links with many disability organisations and is a leading thinker on social policy issues affecting disabled people. He is a trustee of a number of charities including Motability and is a governor of Liverpool John Moores University. He was a founding Commissioner on the Equality and Human Rights Commission and has his own consultancy business, Bert Massie Ltd. He also chairs the internet job search company BeMyNextJob plc. He was appointed a CBE in 2000 and created a knight in 2007.

"This Code of Practice is as welcome as it is timely. For the uninitiated, it might appear lengthy. It is clear, however, that the Code has been meticulously thought through. It could only have been compiled and written by somebody with great experience of the ins and outs, the twists and turns and sometimes the perversities of community equipment provision. Its length is in fact proportionate to the subject matter, not too voluminous yet not so short as to be superficial. It has substance.

The Code does more than just unravel a complex system. It demonstrates time and again that effective and timely provision of community equipment meets key priorities of central government in health and social care - in particular, prevention of problems, independence of the individual and cost effectiveness. In addition, it highlights the legal consequences of not adhering to the good practice it sets out.

Current government policy talks of choice, control and personalisation for service users. Laudable aims, they come also with a risk attached, especially at a time of financial crisis in public services. This risk is that we could be pitched into a modern day Wild West where shortcuts are taken and anything goes. In this respect the Code performs a crucial function.

Whether applied to more traditional or more innovative models of equipment provision, the Code is a reminder of the basics: rights, responsibilities and safety. Without these, talk of choice, control and improved quality of life for people in need will prove hollow.

Twenty three years ago, I wrote a book called 'How to get equipment for disability', which looked at the system of community equipment provision. Stumbling in the dark and with a weak torch so to speak, I struggled to make sense of it. Now, in contrast, Brian Donnelly has commendably and expertly trained a powerful search beam on community equipment and put it into sharp relief. I am in no doubt that the Code he has written will prove to be an invaluable and practical tool."

Michael Mandelstam MSc

Michael Mandelstam MSc is a leading writer and adviser on social and health care law. Michael has worked for the Disabled Living Foundation and the Department of Health; he has also produced a wealth of books and support material on community care related legal issues, including community equipment. He currently works independently, running legal training courses throughout the United Kingdom for NHS Trusts, Local Authorities and voluntary organisations.

x

Preface

Health and social care services in England are going through a time of unprecedented change, with the Government's proposals for the National Health Service (NHS), as set out in the White Paper *Equity and Excellence: Liberating the NHS* and its Vision for Adult Social Care *Capable Communities and Active Citizens*. Notable changes include the introduction of an NHS Commissioning Board, GP commissioning and the formation of Health and Wellbeing Boards.

There has never been a greater time of need for efficiency and productivity in public services, whilst simultaneously improving the quality of care, and complying with the range of legal duties and obligations[1] surrounding health and social care[2] services.

To meet some of the challenges ahead, there is a greater focus on integrated care and partnerships for commissioning, as well as working together with community based support from across the sectors[3].

The NHS Commissioning Board will have a duty to promote partnership working. The newly formed Health and Wellbeing Boards, supported by the Local Authority managed Public Health service, will be expected to consider how to meet the identified needs of the whole local community (using Joint Strategic Needs Assessments), and to develop strategies to tackle the wider determinants of health and wellbeing, e.g. work, mobility, education and housing.

Therefore, the Boards will be tasked with agreeing strategic priorities for meeting local needs and this will include consideration of how pooled funding and joint working arrangements can be used to promote effective commissioning to improve services at the front line.

---

[1] For example, UN Convention on the Rights of Disabled People, The Equality Act 2010, The Health and Safety (Offences) Act 2008.

[2] Adult social care legislation is currently under review and is subject to change.

[3] See *Think Local, Act Personal. A sector-wide commitment to moving forward with personalisation and community based support* January 2011.

GP commissioners will need to publish a Local Commissioning Plan submitted to the NHS Commissioning Board and prepared through discussion and commentary from the Health and Wellbeing Board.

How services are being provided is also changing, with a variety of service delivery models emerging from across the sectors, including the independent and private sector, supported by the growing emphasis for the 'any willing qualified provider' policy to be applied to NHS funded care outside of hospitals.

It is a critical time for ensuring the health and wellbeing of the service user is not put at risk through planning for policy implementation or budgetary constraints, and that the responsibility and accountability of health and Local Authority commissioners and providers do not get lost during service transformation.

These issues are particularly relevant for the provision of community equipment, as this pivotal service has a role to play across the health and social care spectrum, and falls within the remit of both Local Authority and NHS bodies with a common interest and offering a common gain.

Like many other services, the provision of community equipment is in desperate need of protection and investment. Here, community equipment provision has the potential to avoid huge costs elsewhere in the health and social care system, if properly commissioned, managed and funded; it is hoped that this is something that commissioners are beginning to grasp.

Why is community equipment important, and why does it have an essential role in these challenging times?

Most equipment issued by the public sector is issued by local community equipment services, of which there are 138 providers in England. Most of these are run jointly by Local Authorities and the NHS. Equipment is also provided by special schools, hospitals, care homes and third sector organisations.

The spectrum of community equipment provision is broad, meeting, for example, therapeutic, mobility, communication, educational, environmental, independence, prevention and rehabilitation needs. Equipment can be provided for use in the home, school, work, or for social purposes.

If commissioned and managed appropriately, the provision of community equipment offers the potential to cut unscheduled hospital admissions, cut Accident and Emergency attendance, reduce the length of hospital stay and assist with the delivery of many quality outcomes for children and adults.

Community equipment is essential for reducing 'bed blocking' in hospitals. It plays a pivotal role in assisting with funding of long term care by avoiding the need for care home admissions and can improve early years development, for example. It is also fundamental in the delivery of early intervention and prevention strategies, and for avoiding crisis admissions to high cost services.

The provision of community equipment for children, older people and people with disabilities is vital in promoting their independence, safety, social inclusion and quality of life, and helps to give people control over their own lives.

Public sector community equipment services issue approximately 9 million pieces of community equipment to 3.2 million service users every year in England. It has been demonstrated in a recent independent study that a 1% failure rate in the provision of equipment and adaptations, which results in a secondary episode of care, e.g. care home or hospital admission, costs the English health and social care economy a potential **£5 billion per annum**[4]. This demonstrates the potential for significant savings to be achieved.

When reviewing statutory provision of community equipment the Audit Commission commented 'If a medicine was discovered with a similar cost-profile, it would be hailed as the wonder drug of the age'[5].

This Code of Practice has been developed with the above issues in mind; it sets down a quality framework for procurement and provision of services, allowing high quality, efficient and safe services to be delivered, with improved clinical

---

[4] Donnelly, B. (2009). *The Need for National Minimum Standards: An Independent Review*. Available at: www.communityequipment.org.uk

[5] Audit Commission (2000 & 2002). *Fully Equipped*: London.

and financial outcomes. The Code provides a foundation for the maintenance and development of service provision in the light of prospective changes; it has been designed to withstand the test of time.

The Community Equipment Code of Practice Scheme (www.cecops.org.uk) has been set up to administer the registration and compliance of all organisations in the community equipment sector who are applying the Code.

Brian Donnelly
June 2011

Acknowledgements

The author would like to thank the following individuals and organisations:

Members of the UK Community Equipment Standards Adoption Group, who have been long-standing supporters of the case for standards to be applied to the community equipment industry; the Welsh Assembly Government for granting permission to use some material the author previously developed for the Welsh National Minimum Standards, when writing this Code of Practice; Naomi Donnelly and Allan Mears for the many hours spent copy-editing and proofreading the content of this Code of Practice; Dr Sue Hurrell for providing a picture of her lovely daughter Imogen for the front cover; Sir Bert Massie CBE, Michael Mandelstam and Robin Lorimer for their valuable support and contributions.

About the Community Equipment Code of Practice Scheme

This book is the official reference guide for the Community Equipment Code of Practice Scheme. Organisations wishing to apply the Code of Practice need to register with the Scheme at: www.cecops.org.uk. Code of Practice registrants will be listed on an online register, and will be granted the right to display appropriate certification marks.

The Code of Practice Scheme is administered and appropriately controlled to maintain its reputation as the quality indicator for the sector. Without the requirement to register with the Scheme, the Code of Practice could become subject to misuse, bringing disrepute to the Scheme, and to those organisations who legitimately comply with the Code of Practice.

A summary explanation of how the Scheme works, including registration and accreditation, is provided in the following paragraphs; further details appear on the Scheme's website.

Why is a Code of Practice needed?

Until the Audit Commission undertook reviews of statutory community equipment services in 2000 and 2002, very little was understood about the importance of providing community equipment. The Audit Commission's reports highlighted systemic failures with commissioning, health and safety aspects, and quality issues which were directly impacting upon other health and social care services. A further review in 2009 highlighted that little improvement had been made since the Audit Commission papers, and called on the need for National Minimum Standards[6] to be introduced. This review was widely received and supported across the industry.

For a service area of such a scale and complexity, and with such an important role to play in support of health and social care, it is surprising that historically there has not been a statutory requirement in England for a minimum standard of service, either in the form of National Minimum Standards, or as a Code of

---

[6] Donnelly, B. (2009). *The Need for National Minimum Standards: An Independent Review*. Available at: www.communityequipment.org.uk

Practice for the sector. This Code of Practice has been developed in response to the overwhelming support from the sector for some form of governing principles to be applied to community equipment related services.

A Code of Practice is an orderly collection of rules, guidelines, standards and other information relating to the recommended practices and procedures to be followed.

The Code of Practice for Community Equipment has been developed specifically for the following reasons:

- to provide practical guidance on how services or functions are commissioned and provided
- to enable compliance with relevant legislation, including statutory duties and obligations
- to set a standard of best industry practice
- to provide a quality framework for commissioners and providers
- to help achieve best value when commissioning or providing services
- to allow services to be assessed against a common benchmark
- to assist commissioners and service users in identifying quality service providers
- to provide a level of assurance to commissioners, providers and service users
- to support the improvement of health related and financial outcomes.

Adherence to the Code of Practice will also provide a good degree of protection for commissioners, provider organisations, service users, carers and others, by ensuring services provided are of an acceptable standard despite pressures which are inevitable through structural change and funding restrictions.

The Code of Practice also supports current policy and regulatory requirements and objectives, such as:

1. Supports the intended responsibilities of the *NHS Commissioning Board*, e.g.:

    i.   promotes integration

    ii. provides leadership for quality improvement through commissioning by standardisation of known best practice

    iii. encourages quality outcomes, good financial performance and productivity through effective commissioning.

2. Aligns with and supports the range of *GP consortia responsibilities and functions,* in relation to: planning, agreeing and monitoring services; improving quality of primary care; financial duties; governance; specific duties of co-operation, and standard duties that fall on relevant public bodies.

3. Fits within the Department of Health led *Quality, Innovation, Productivity and Prevention (QIPP) programme,* by providing good quality and timely community equipment provision, whether it is for enabling a service user to be safely discharged from hospital, prevented from going into hospital in the first place, or being cared for at home.

4. Supports the overall objectives of the *NHS Outcomes Framework* relating to effectiveness, patient experience and safety; together with addressing the *National Institute for health and Clinical Excellence's (NICE)* three dimensions of quality standards: clinical effectiveness, patient safety and patient experience.

5. Complies with *Care Quality Commission* work relating to the essential standards of quality and safety to be expected.

6. Provides a 'ready-made' framework for all commissioners, providers and users of services. It will help both with assessing the needs and developing the strategy of the *Health and Wellbeing Boards*.

The status of the Code of Practice

The Code of Practice is recognised and endorsed by the National Association of Equipment Providers (NAEP) as the official Code of Practice for commissioners and providers of community equipment. The standards set out within this Code of Practice have also been commended by many of the leading professional membership bodies, associations, regulators and third sector organisations operating within the community equipment sector.

Commissioning and providing bodies are expected to fulfil their statutory duties towards those with an assessed equipment need. This Code of Practice gives effective guidance in the fulfilment of those statutory duties; **it does not impose further duties**.

The Code of Practice is designed to aid effective decisions but it does not, and could not, prescribe exactly what to do in each individual case. The duty to have regard to this Code of Practice will continue for its lifetime. The Code of Practice will be updated regularly to reflect changes in policy, strategy and legislation.

All commissioners and providers of community equipment, including health, social services and education authorities, and providers to these organisations, are advised to respect this Code of Practice as it has been developed to aid the provision of these services in keeping with quality standards and relevant duties and legislation.

The scope of the Code of Practice

The Code of Practice applies in some measure to all areas where equipment is commissioned and provided in the community. Although statutory health and social care community equipment stores provide the majority of equipment into the community, there are also a number of other relevant means of provision and settings for community equipment, e.g. continuing healthcare equipment, equipment issued to children in special schools, and care homes. The Code of Practice will have different applications depending upon the environment, types of equipment and quantity provided.

The Code of Practice also covers the Department of Health led 'Transforming Community Equipment Services' (TCES) Retail Model. Where appropriate, the Code of Practice provides guidance on dealing with ambiguous aspects of the Retail Model, such as statutory and retailer responsibilities.

In terms of overall scope, the Code of Practice applies to *all* the various means of statutory provision, and where this document refers to 'community equipment provision', this includes all the sources of statutory provision.

How the Code of Practice Scheme works

The Code of Practice Scheme is overseen and controlled by a not-for-profit organisation - for further details visit: www.cecops.org.uk. Officeholders of this organisation include prominent figures from across the industry.

1. Registration

Organisations can use or apply the Code of Practice in whole or in part, and doing so are required to register under the Scheme.

There are three categories of registration, *Full*, *Associate*, and *Affiliate*, depending upon the level of involvement with community equipment. To find out which category is applicable to your organisation visit the Scheme website: www.cecops.org.uk.

Within these categories, there are two levels of application, depending on how many parts of the Code will apply to your organisation. The two levels are:

    i. **Entry Level** – this entitles users to work to any *two* of the main Parts of the Code of Practice.

    ii. **Enhanced Level** - this entitles users to work to *all four* Parts of the Code of Practice.

Registered users will be awarded a Certificate of Registration, and will be listed on the User Register, publicly available online.

2. Accreditation

Registered users will be required to self-monitor their compliance with the Code of Practice. However, for reasons of credibility it is recommended that Accreditation is sought. Accreditation involves external assessment of a registered user's compliance with the Code of Practice.

Benefits of applying for Accreditation include:

- gives an organisation an independent assessment of how well it complies with the Code of Practice
- gives assurance to commissioning organisations that their commissioning practices are of a good standard

- Enables commissioners and service users to identify organisations which have been independently verified as meeting the standards set out within the Code of Practice
- Gives provider organisations a competitive advantage by having independent verification that they meet the standards set out in the Code of Practice.

An independent auditing body will carry out assessments, using an agreed Audit Programme to assess organisations against the requirements of the Code of Practice.

Following a satisfactory assessment outcome, an organisation will be awarded a Certificate of Accreditation, and will be listed as an Accredited User on the online Register.

It is desirable for organisations to obtain accreditation, as this demonstrates that service quality has been externally verified. It could also be used for satisfying regulators, marketing purposes, or demonstrating best value, for example.

3. Training

Most organisations wishing to apply the Code of Practice will require training to ensure they are able to comply with it. Under the Code of Practice Scheme, courses will be available from Accredited Trainers; these individuals and organisations will themselves have undergone rigorous training, to gain their accreditation. Accredited Trainers will work to an agreed training programme to ensure consistency across the country.

Details of Accredited Trainers will be available on the Scheme's website: www.cecops.org.uk. Training will be available to cover all aspects of equipment provision, including commissioning, provision and related clinical responsibilities.

Who can use the Code of Practice?

The Code of Practice can be used by any organisation or individual responsible for commissioning or providing community equipment. It will also be useful to other organisations which are associated with community equipment, but do not have commissioning or providing responsibilities.

It will be noticed that the principles set out in this Code of Practice could be applicable to other equipment related services, e.g. wheelchair services, communication equipment, telehealth, and those involved in these services may wish to work to the Code of Practice. However it should be noted that as this Code of Practice has not been specifically developed for other services, its application in these cases will necessarily be limited, and there may be gaps in coverage.

Use of the Code of Practice is permitted by other types of service, but accreditation would not be possible due to potential limitations in applicability of the Code. Anyone wishing to apply the Code of Practice to other services should register as for community equipment service provision.

The Code of Practice may in the future be extended or adapted to cover specifically other services, or other parts of the UK, and the author would appreciate any comments or input from any individual or organisation interested in being involved with this.

Introduction

The provision of community equipment is complex, and is an essential part of many care related public services. However, many core functions of equipment services are similar, regardless of the means of provision, and establishing common ground rules for all sources of provision is invaluable in managing this essential service area. This Code of Practice has been designed to be used right across the spectrum of provision as a tool to enable services to be appropriately commissioned, provided, monitored and assessed.

The Code of Practice is supported by various stakeholders from across the industry, e.g. clinical professional bodies, regulators, third sector organisations and independent advisory agencies, etc. The Code has also been officially endorsed by the National Association of Equipment Providers (NAEP) as the recognised standards organisations and services should be working to.

The Code of Practice aligns with current legislative duties and powers, including, for example, the United Nations Convention on the Rights of Disabled People, Health and Safety (Offences) Act 2008.

The Code of Practice goes beyond the traditional scope of community equipment provision. For example, over many years provision of equipment has been perceived as a procurement function, with significant focus on the efficient provision of specific items. When applying the Social Model of Disability it becomes apparent that the provision of equipment is a means of eliminating environmental barriers to independence. The Code of Practice adopts the Social Model of Disability principles, compliance with which will result in much wider and more sustainable outlying benefits, e.g. access to education, in addition to more immediate health and social care benefits.

In view of current and future changes to how services are commissioned, it is important that the Code of Practice is used as a tool to enable a seamless transition. This will ensure service provision of community equipment does not slip through the net during times of organisational change. Partnership and pooled funding arrangements can continue between health services and Local Authorities, and other strategic partners, as encouraged within health and wellbeing strategies, and this Code of Practice supports these arrangements.

This Code of Practice provides a quality framework for ensuring risks, governance and health and safety duties, obligations and standards are clearly specified by commissioners and understood by providing organisations. The Code will also provide an appropriate guide for monitoring and assessing the overall performance of the commissioner and provider respectively.

Note. Although there is a 'clinical' focus in some parts of the Code of Practice, which in some cases can imply a 'medical' model, this does not exclude or lessen the social care aspects of provision including, for example, providers, assessors and prescribers.

Part 1: Commissioning and Governance

Introduction to Code standards 1 to 8

To ensure the needs of the service user are met, and the right outcomes are achieved, the importance of commissioning, or planning, and governance should not be underestimated, in relation to the provision of community equipment.

Generally speaking community equipment providers will only respond to the requirements set out by those commissioning or planning the service. In view of this it is important for commissioners to understand fully the needs and views of the service user; this can be done for example by service user representation on the Health and Wellbeing Boards, and in the development of relevant strategy.

Although service users undoubtedly benefit from professional advice, it is equally important to recognise that they also have expertise with regard to the challenges they face on a daily basis, and the help that they need. It is vital that they also contribute to assessment and review processes.

Not only is it important to ensure services are properly commissioned, it is equally important to have systems in place to ensure what is being specified by the commissioners is actually being delivered by the provider, and thus the outcome is being achieved. Therefore good commissioning, governance, procurement and contract management arrangements for the provision of community equipment are crucial.

If the service levels and quality of community equipment provision are poor, this can sometimes be due to the absence of relevant data and information contained in the original service specifications and contracts. This can result in a poor standard of quality being achieved, poor outcomes for the service user, and in some cases can be more expensive than originally intended. Specifying service requirements poorly can also significantly impact upon other health and social care services, and can affect long term partnership working, for example.

Without providing the right level of information, e.g. activity data, within service specifications or contracts, etc. it is very likely that services will be inadequately funded. Without adequate funding inappropriate decisions relating to eligibility criteria can arise, which will ultimately be to the detriment of the service user, and may even cause some services to fall into illegal practice.

When specifying service requirements it is not advisable to use general statements about legal and welfare obligations, e.g. 'the provider must comply with all relevant health and safety requirements'. It is important for commissioners to specify in detail the actual legal and welfare related obligations the provider is expected to comply with, as it is all too easy for assumptions to be made about what service providers should be doing.

It is equally important for the provider of services to know from the outset the parameters that they are expected to work within, especially as they may need to bid for more resources to comply with all the obligations placed upon them. For example, by specifying that a provider should comply with the Provision and Use of Work Equipment Regulations 1998 (PUWER), this necessarily requires the provider to comply with manufacturers' instructions which, in turn, may require more funding and staffing resources for on-going maintenance and replacement of parts.

Furthermore it is important for service users to be aware of the level of service to expect. This might be in the form of a Patient's Charter, or similar information package.

In view of the above issues it is very important to note that it is entirely the responsibility of those commissioning the provision of community equipment to ensure the right information is specified and communicated, and equally that the right controls are in place to ensure requirements, expectations, and outcomes can be measured and are being achieved.

The following list outlines some of the overarching legislation and treaties which directly apply to the commissioning of community equipment. Each of these places a significant responsibility and in some cases a duty upon commissioners (and providers), and all can have serious consequences, if breached. The following list, together with local policies should be considered by those commissioning and/or planning community equipment provision (this list is not exhaustive):

- UN Convention on the Rights of Disabled People[7]
- UN Convention on the Rights of the Child
- Corporate Manslaughter Act 2007
- The Health and Safety (Offences) Act 2008
- The Equality Act 2010
- Human Rights Act 1998 (European Convention on Human Rights)
- Common law of negligence
- Health and Safety at Work Act etc 1974
- Management of Health and Safety at Work Regulations 1999
- Manual Handling Operations Regulations 1992
- Lifting Operations and Lifting Equipment Regulations 1998
- Provision and Use of Work Equipment Regulations 1998
- Health and Social Care Act 2008
- NHS Act 2006
- NHS and Community Care Act 1990
- Chronically Sick and Disabled Persons Act 1970.

To view the full legal and welfare framework relating to community equipment provision see Appendix 1. Note that the above list is only an example of relevant legislation at the time of writing. Neither is it intended to be an exhaustive list. As legislation is subject to change it is recommended to keep up to date with current legislation.

---

[7] This Convention is known as 'The Rights of Persons with Disabilities' in other parts of the United Nations. The Office for Disability Issues chose to retitle the Convention for its use in the UK.

CODE STANDARD 1

Service Requirements and Specifications

OUTCOME

The requirements and expectations for the delivery of a community equipment service are clearly specified and communicated, realistic, and easy to be interpreted and understood.

Introduction to Code standard 1

Without the provider of community equipment, including retailers, having a clear understanding about what it is they are expected by the commissioners to do, in terms of service requirements and outcomes, it is very likely that problems will arise. Clearly specifying service expectations and standards, mutually negotiated and agreed to, and having the right controls and measures in place for ensuring compliance, are key in the delivery of an all-round successful community equipment service.

1.1 The commissioners have clearly specified their service requirements in the form of a service level agreement, service specification and/or a contract, as appropriate.

1.2 The commissioners have clearly specified their actual and realistic requirements in terms of approximate numbers, activity levels, together with agreed tolerances, etc. The contractual agreement specifies the procedure to be taken should activity levels exceed or fall below these tolerances.

1.3 The commissioners have agreed with the provider prior to commencing the contract that the requirements and expectations placed upon the provider are realistic, and have been arrived at using an appropriate calculated formula. Where there is no historic or suitable data available to form such an agreement (i.e. when a completely new service is being set up) frequent reviews are agreed with the provider to monitor and assess activities.

1.4 The commissioners have not used general and vague statements within their service specification and/or contract, etc. where ambiguity could be to the detriment of service provision. For example, requesting that the provider complies with all relevant health and safety requirements is too broad, and could be misleading. Providers should be given a comprehensive list setting out actual requirements and obligations, e.g. 'a portable appliance test is carried out on all portable electrical appliances in accordance with the Electricity at Work Regulations 1989.'

1.5 Service level agreements/service specifications and/or contracts are reviewed at fixed intervals, e.g. annually, and reviews involve suitable stakeholders and users of the services.

1.6 The commissioners have clearly set out a Patient's Charter, or similar information package, outlining the levels of service to expect. This is particularly important where retail sources are used as part of provision.

1.7 There is a list of the equipment types that are provided under statutory provision; this includes both simple and complex aids. Any approved retailers also have access to this list.

1.8 The commissioners have clearly specified roles, responsibilities and accountabilities between them and retailers; this is particularly important where the retailer upgrades/upsells the prescription item. As a minimum there is a Memorandum of Understanding in place between the commissioner and the retailer.

CODE STANDARD 2

Partnerships, Joint Working and Pooled Funding

OUTCOME

Sector-wide integrated commissioning and joint working is in place, together with pooled funding arrangements (where appropriate) to ensure duplication and inefficiency are minimised.

Introduction to Code standard 2

There are many statutory organisations funding delivery of similar community based equipment related services, e.g. health, Local Authority (Housing, Education and Social Care). Some of these may also provide services directly themselves (i.e. in-house), or have separate arrangements for access to the funded services.

In view of the scope for duplication, time delays and inefficiencies when providing entirely separate services for the same service user, efforts have been made over recent years to improve integration and joint working between these organisations.

These organisations are also able to integrate commissioning for services through, for example, pooling their funds using Section 75 of the National Health Service Act 2006.

They (NHS commissioners and Local Authorities - LAs) may also make direct grants from one to the other on the grounds that granting say, NHS funds to a LA for it to meet more LA responsibilities is a more effective use of public funds than if the NHS money were used directly upon NHS care.

The grant arrangements are known as Section 256 and Section 76 of the NHS Act 2006 (previously known as Section 28A and Section 28B). These are a simpler form of integrating funding but essentially an arrangement where the two agencies agree what the objectives for the grant to be used by the recipient are as an addition to their own funding. This is not a partnership but is a useful mechanism for one partner to increase the resources of the other having recognised the benefit of doing so locally.

The two agencies can then, through these routes to joint working, create a single collective funding source to secure services from others.

There are many voluntary and private sector organisations, and wider support services, such as housing agencies, providing equipment related functions. As yet the benefits of these organisations and sectors fully engaging in joint working for seamless, timely and cost effective equipment supply have not been fully explored and realised.

There is now greater potential to bring these service providers closer, as partnership and joint working across the sectors is part of the Government's vision for Adult Social Care, and the NHS: *'Capable Communities and Active Citizens'*, November 2010, and *'Think Local, Act Personal. A sector-wide commitment to moving forward with personalisation and community based support'* January 2011, and as set out in the White Paper *'Equity and Excellence: Liberating the NHS'*.

Also, Health and Wellbeing Boards have a duty to promote integrated working between health and social care commissioners. They are also expected to promote joint working with commissioners of services which impact on wider health determinants, e.g. education and housing.

2.1 There are formal agreements in place for funding, integrated commissioning and joint delivery of working service arrangements between NHS and Local Authorities responsible for arranging community equipment locally.

2.2 Where there is a Section 75 formal partnership in place, this will comprise a written document covering the 'flexibilities' being used, e.g. lead commissioning and/or integrated delivery.

2.3 The available Section 75 agreements include (but are not limited to):

- names of statutory partners (these can only be NHS and LA)
- purpose of the agreement
- date and duration of agreement
- which (Health Act) flexibilities apply
- the aims, outcomes and targets set by the partnership or commissioning body (this may be available within the Health and Wellbeing Board's overall strategy)
- who the service users are/who the service is for. This is defined in terms of service user group, age range, LA, NHS and partner areas, etc.
- how the services are to be accessed, e.g. assessment and eligibility
- how much resource is to be committed to the partnership by each commissioning partner and any organisational services in support of the partnership, e.g. information, premises, procurement support

- how resources are changed, especially the budget building exercise for future years
- how the agreement is managed, e.g. joint governance group to set annual plans and targets, monitor performance, agree variations, manage reviews/renewal, and reporting to others
- when the agreement is subject to review, and frequency of reviews
- how performance is measured.

2.4 There is evidence of good working relationships between the different organisations and sectors involved in the provision of community equipment. (There might also be other arrangements outside of direct Section 75 arrangements, e.g. acute hospitals and third sector organisations working collaboratively, even where there is no formal partnership agreement or pooled funding in place. Similarly the possibility of shared funding between charitable organisations acting 'in consortia' is to be considered alongside private funding (top-ups), regional and local statutory services).

2.5 Partnerships of any form are able to offer transparent evidence of their processes for co-ordination of service provision that reflects a person centred approach to meeting people's 'whole-life' needs.

2.6 Personalisation and direct payments are considered in the planning and arrangements for support with obtaining local personal services. These initiatives are not inhibited by partnerships for equipment.

CODE STANDARD 3

Funding Arrangements

OUTCOME

Services are adequately funded in relation to requirements and expectations.

Introduction to Code standard 3

Funding for community equipment can be problematic; this is often due to the relationship between activity and cost not being fully understood. If services are inappropriately funded significant problems can arise for the provider of services, and can result in dangerous and even illegal practice. This is especially true where services have to take 'shortcuts' in service standards, in order to operate within the funds allocated to them. Not only can inappropriate funding result in risk issues, it may actually cost the wider health and social care economy more in the longer term by having to fund more costly episodes of care, e.g. more people being admitted to hospitals and care homes.

3.1 Service providers are appropriately funded to enable them to meet the requirements of their service specifications and any policy and regulatory requirements.

3.2 There are clear and agreed activity tolerance levels providers are expected to operate within.

3.3 There is a clear formula in place demonstrating how funding allocations have been calculated; an impact assessment is provided in the case where equipment provision is not adequately funded, or if funding is withdrawn.

3.4 Funding allocations are not based entirely upon previous budgets and/or spend, but match what the provider is actually being asked to undertake for the relevant period. Retrospective funding may be necessary in some instances, where for example a new service has been set up, i.e. in the absence of sufficient data to allocate funds, funding can be allocated after running the service for an agreed period.

3.5 A schedule is available showing a breakdown of activities and related costs, e.g. deliveries, collections, maintenance. A breakdown of expenditure for different elements of equipment is available, e.g. simple aids to daily living, complex and children's equipment. Where relevant, expenditure breakdown also covers retail provision for simple aids.

3.6 Where appropriate, funding includes whole-life costs for equipment, e.g. maintenance, replacement parts. Where top-ups via retailers are encouraged, or where direct payments are awarded, there is clarity over whole-life costs, i.e. who is responsible for maintenance and replacing broken parts, post sales.

3.7 Community equipment providers have been actively involved in providing costs for the running of operations. This may be through the submission of a pre-purchase questionnaire, or similar mechanism.

3.8 Expenditure on all specific categories of equipment is monitored whether or not equipment is integrated or pooled. This includes a breakdown of amounts paid to retailers supplying under the Retail Model, where appropriate.

CODE STANDARD 4

Contractual Arrangements

OUTCOME

Community equipment provision is subject to formal contracting arrangements, and documentation is in place which has clear terms and conditions, with roles and responsibilities specified. This includes a clear service specification.

Introduction to Code standard 4

In the past there have been cases where community equipment has been provided without formal contractual arrangements being in place; this is partly owing to services being in-house and having evolved over the years. As more services are provided through partnership and other integrated arrangements, together with the outsourcing of some service provision, service specifications and contractual arrangements are now more commonly required and beneficial to use.

Without a formal contractual arrangement in place it is difficult to conceive how service providers can deliver an efficient service. Efficiency presumes specification outcomes and targets that are measurable and, above all, achievable.

For regional areas which have adopted the TCES Retail Model for the provision of simple aids, or a 'hybrid' equipment model, it is equally important to have contracts, or, as a minimum, a 'Memorandum of Understanding' in place. A 'Memorandum of Understanding' is an agreement between two parties. It is not fully binding in the way that a contract is, but it is stronger and more formal than a verbal agreement.

Where the TCES Model is being used for the provision of simple aids, complex aids will either be provided in-house or by a third party. This may mean that it could be more difficult to manage the various contracts for equipment provision.

4.1 Services are provided through contract arrangements (using an internal Service Level Agreement (SLA) for non-contracted out services), dependent upon whether services are provided by internal or external providers.

4.2 Where there is integrated provision, formal partnership working is in evidence by a formal partnership agreement.

4.3 Where there are several independent providers, commissioned to provide the full service, they can demonstrate co-operation between each other and across the service user pathway.

4.4 Commissioners clearly set out the roles and responsibilities for each of the respective organisations, and key individuals involved.

4.5 Contracts and/or formal agreements carry local legal endorsement.

CODE STANDARD 5

Legal and Welfare Obligations
OUTCOME
The legal and welfare requirements, including individual and organisational duties and responsibilities, relating to the provision of community equipment, are clearly documented.

Introduction to Code standard 5

The legal and welfare duties, obligations and parameters for the provision of community equipment are extensive – see Appendix 1. These are in place to protect the service user, staff and organisations alike. Duties and obligations could unknowingly be breached without appropriate measures in place to ensure compliance.

In essence there are three types of obligation as shown by the following diagram:

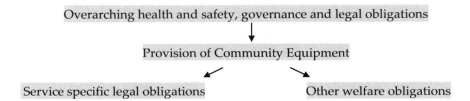

It is very important for commissioners, providers, professionals and end users of the service to be clear about the particular legal and welfare related duties and obligations that pertain to them; otherwise assumptions could be made about who is responsible, which sometimes results in significant breaches.

5.1 The legal and welfare boundaries that providers of community equipment are expected to operate within are clearly identified and written into all Memoranda of Understanding, service level agreements, service specifications, contract agreements, and/or partnership agreements, as appropriate.

5.2 Information relating to legal and welfare obligations is communicated effectively, and in appropriate formats, to all responsible individuals and organisations highlighting their specific responsibilities.

5.3 Information is available to service users setting out their legal entitlement to community equipment. This may be in the form of a Patient's Charter, for example.

Author's note:

Care needs to be exercised when considering the legal and welfare duties and obligations set out within this document. The legislation provided is relevant at the time of writing this Code of Practice; it is not exhaustive and is only intended to be a general guide. Commissioners are advised to seek the advice of legal departments within their own organisation.

Furthermore, the various legal requirements set out in this Code have not restated wider organisational responsibilities which may indirectly apply, e.g. Data Protection Act 1998. The intended purpose of setting out the list of legal and welfare duties and obligations within the Code is to signpost to legislation which is mostly relevant to community equipment provision.

CODE STANDARD 6

Governance and Risk Management

OUTCOME

Clear and comprehensive governance and risk management strategies exist, covering all aspects of service delivery, whilst ensuring appropriate reporting mechanisms and controls are in place for monitoring purposes.

Introduction to Code standard 6

Currently most community equipment providers are commissioned and governed by health and Local Authority partnership boards or joint management groups. Despite prospective changes to NHS commissioning, these boards or joint management groups will be likely to continue, albeit within a different organisational structure.

The command paper for NHS legislative change envisages that responsibilities for existing Section 75 agreement commitments will transfer to GP consortia, and with the new Health and Wellbeing Boards promoting additional new integration opportunities to secure joint services to meet local needs.

It is a requirement of the Health and Wellbeing Strategy to consider the continued use of pooled funding and partnership arrangements.

Section 75 Health Act 2006 flexibilities for pooled funding arrangements between NHS and LAs need to be applied appropriately, regardless of whether the services are jointly managed in-house or outsourced through contracts with others.

The responsibilities of joint boards and groups established to oversee partnerships are very broad. They will have the ultimate responsibility and overall accountability for ensuring all governance and risk issues are managed appropriately, e.g. quality; performance; risks; finances; contractual arrangements, and clinical governance. Without the presence of this formal governance structure service provision could become ineffective, inefficient and unsafe.

Commissioners are also responsible for ensuring the needs of the service user are met and that the governance of procured services reflects how service user rights and protections are ensured.

It is sometimes assumed that outsourcing certain components of service provision reduces or removes statutory responsibility and accountability, especially for governance and risk management arrangements; this is also sometimes the case where the TCES Retail Model has been adopted. However, commissioners should be clear that in these instances they *retain* the responsibility to ensure governance and risk issues are assessed, communicated and monitored.

It is vital that where the Retail Model has been adopted sufficient safeguards and assurances are in place to ensure statutory responsibilities are still being met. One method of obtaining some assurance is by having a recognised retailer accreditation scheme in place. For example the British Healthcare Trades Association (BHTA) and the National Association of Equipment Providers (NAEP) have jointly developed the nationally recognized Community

Equipment Dispenser Accreditation Body (CEDAB)[8] system, which is used by some organisations which have adopted the Retail Model.

6.1 Governance arrangements are in place and are clearly documented. The documentation outlines specific areas of responsibilities, together with monitoring procedures and named individuals/posts responsible for ensuring procedures are followed.

6.2 Governance arrangements are clearly documented and form part of all contractual arrangements.

6.3 There is a service specific risk management strategy in place which addresses, for example, the accessibility of services[9], prevention of deterioration of conditions and risk to carers, management of care to users, sustaining community living, prevention of hospital admission and life-style choices. This is clearly documented, communicated and understood by all relevant parties. The risk management strategy also includes, but is not limited to, such things as:

- roles and responsibilities of commissioners and providers
- links to other risk related boards e.g. Medical Device Management Board
- medical device management
- health and safety and risk management
- accreditation process of retailers
- exit strategy if the retailer closes, or can no longer provide a service.

6.4 Where a formal partnership agreement exists it incorporates a risk management and risk sharing section specifying processes for identifying and responding to identified risks, alongside partner roles and

---

[8] CEDAB was formed in 2007 to establish the first registration scheme and accreditation body to champion the provision of a quality assured prescription based dispensing service for the Community Equipment Services Retail Model and all retail establishments throughout the United Kingdom.

[9] The Equality Act 2010 requires a disability discrimination impact assessment to be undertaken when developing services. One of the key issues is accessibility. This means a lot more than just having a ramp outside a building. This includes the accessibility of information, the ability to get physically to the service, and access to the physical premises. Accessibility is enshrined in the Equality Act 2010 and also in UN Convention on The Rights of Disabled People.

responsibilities. A risk sharing section relating to finances will also be included.

6.5 A designated and named lead has been appointed within the commissioning body with overall responsibility for medical device management relating to the provision of community equipment.

6.6 The complaints procedure is transparent and easily accessible to people with differing communication needs - advocacy is available where necessary. It separates areas of responsibility and clearly sets out contact details and processes for different aspects of the service, e.g. retail provision. For jointly commissioned services, governed by a partnership agreement, the 'lead' commissioning partner is responsible for ensuring that any contracted providers have adequate complaints arrangements in place and that these are made known to service users at the point of service contact.

CODE STANDARD 7

Eligibility Criteria

OUTCOME

There is clarity over eligibility criteria, and consistency in their use and application.

Introduction to Code standard 7

Issues relating to eligibility criteria can sometimes be problematic, especially in relation to availability of funds to meet the service user's need. These difficulties are likely to increase as financial resources for both the NHS and Local Authorities come under pressure.

Community equipment is usually provided by services integrated between health and social care, and these often have pooled funding arrangements in place.

Difficulty is often presented within integrated provision when attempting to apply unified eligibility criteria for issuing equipment. Quite often these difficulties can result in service users not receiving the equipment they actually need, and, in many case, are entitled to.

There are certain demarcations between health and Local Authority eligibility criteria. For example, under the *Fair Access to Care Services* policy document Local Authorities are required to specify what level of need they will meet in relation to independence, i.e. critical, substantial, moderate or low; this is usually determined by the level of funds available. They are required to specify this at the beginning of the financial year[10].

In contrast, the NHS does not usually specify the level of need it will meet, and can, in some circumstances, refuse to provide equipment where it can be proved that it lacked the financial resources. Where services are integrated with pooled funding arrangements, services should attempt to work toward a unified approach to eligibility criteria in order to avoid confusion and variations in decision making.

Some authorities apply blanket policies on the equipment types they will provide, together with financial threshold restrictions. This may in some instances be contrary to current legislation which requires an assessed need to be met, regardless of the type of equipment or cost. It is also inconsistent with statutory guidance issued by the Department of Health.[11] This practice can result in service users not receiving the appropriate equipment, or indeed, not receiving equipment at all. This type of policy should therefore be avoided.

In view of all these issues, caution needs to be exercised whenever determining eligibility criteria. It should be borne in mind that tightening the eligibility criteria can actually be more costly in the longer term if, for example, not addressing a service user's 'moderate' needs could cause their needs to become 'critical'. Similarly, by not addressing a health need this can become a social care need, and vice versa. Statutory guidance from the Department of Health suggests that whatever a person's eligibility for social care services is judged to

---

[10] Department of Health (2010). *Prioritising need in the context of Putting People First: a whole system approach to eligibility for social care - guidance on eligibility criteria for adult social care, England 2010.*

[11] Department of Health (2010). *Prioritising need in the context of Putting People First: a whole system approach to eligibility for social care - guidance on eligibility criteria for adult social care, England 2010,* paras 19, 62, 124.

be, Local Authorities might anyway wish to give people direct payments for equipment to reduce their needs for further support.[12]

7.1 The decision making process used for equipment provision is based entirely upon, and in accordance with any locally relevant eligibility criteria. The decision is also linked to and based upon the user outcomes (i.e. considering the consequence of not providing equipment).

7.2 The eligibility criteria used for deciding on equipment provision is documented and communicated to all relevant individuals involved in issuing equipment.

7.3 Where organisations have come together by partnership agreement and developed single eligibility criteria, this is publicly available for all staff and service users. Details of eligibility criteria are included in the partnership agreement.

CODE STANDARD 8

Contract and Performance Management

OUTCOME

Contracts are appropriately managed and reviewed to ensure performance is optimal, and this is evidenced sufficiently to meet audit requirements.

Introduction to Code standard 8

Management of contracts with service providers is an area that can be easily overlooked or taken for granted. Without effective contract management arrangements in place it is almost certain that good performance standards will be lacking. Contract management responsibilities should be assigned to named individuals, in order to keep a close rein on all the different aspects of the service.

---

[12] Department of Health (2009). *Guidance on direct payments for community care, services for carers and children's services*, para 107.

It is important that robust and meaningful indicators are used to capture and ascertain performance levels; there are many performance indicators available to support this. It is equally important to ensure that the means for collecting the data are robust, e.g. IT systems, especially where audit is concerned.

Where authorities have adopted the TCES Retail Model for the provision of simple aids it is also important to ensure that relevant performance related issues can be captured. This might be done for example by having systems and processes in place for monitoring the number of prescriptions issued; how many were redeemed, and when they were redeemed.

It is reported that a significant number of prescriptions issued under the TCES Retail Model are never redeemed. If this is the case it is important to have a system in place to track when and why this might be happening. It might also be necessary to establish whether this has occurred because the service user does not want the equipment and can cope without it, or whether the service user is too unwell physically to collect the equipment. Failure to track and follow up unredeemed prescriptions could mean that the most vulnerable are not getting a service, and that they end up requiring other, more costly, care provision.

8.1 Those with commissioning responsibilities have robust contract and performance management measures in place for ensuring optimum contract performance is achieved, which also reflect user satisfaction. The table in Appendix 2 sets out a guide to some of the more general contract management indicators that can be used for measuring performance. Other local measures can be used in addition.

8.2 Commissioners are informed about contract performance by reliable management reports.

8.3 In order to ensure contracts are appropriately managed there is a designated lead individual with overall contract management responsibilities.

8.4 Performance is ascertained by various methods, for example, relevant Key Performance Indicators (KPIs), contract management and relevant quality measures. Local measures and indicators may also be in place, especially with retailers.

8.5 The performance measures in place satisfy pertinent audit and inspection purposes, in terms of data collection processes, validation, robustness and accuracy.

8.6 Relevant performance data is captured electronically from internal IT systems, as manual collection of data will not generally meet auditors' requirements.

8.7 Key Performance Indicator reports record all deliveries and collections of equipment and adaptations, etc. Where relevant the reports also show activity with retailers.

8.8 Performance reports also include reasons for failure and, where relevant, unredeemed prescriptions.

8.9 Where appropriate, all reporting on performance reflects integrated provision, e.g. health and social care. Services may however still wish to break down individual health and social care performance to suit local requirements. Regardless of the number of providers and third party contractors supplying different aspects of service delivery, management reports are available to demonstrate individual and collective performance.

8.10 Where service provision involves different providers for different types of equipment, e.g. retailers for simple aids and outsourced providers for beds and hoists, performance is combined into one legible and meaningful report.

8.11 Where an arrangement is set up with retailers to provide simple aids there is a written, and mutually agreed, understanding about performance and contractual obligations.

8.12 There is a nominated individual within the commissioning body with governance responsibility for ensuring the providing organisation's IT system, and the information provided by the system, are robust. An authorisation process is in place to ensure no significant changes can be made to the system without the prior approval of this individual.

Part 2: Service Provision

Introduction to Code standards 9 to 23

The provision of community equipment involves a broad range of functions, e.g. providing a stores facility, procurement, logistics, delivery and collection of equipment, decontamination and maintenance, equipment installation; along with offering a clinical support service. Very often community equipment providers are required to support multi-agency, integrated and pooled funding arrangements, usually involving both health and social care partners. The provision of community equipment therefore has many interfaces, with many expectations and obligations to fulfil.

Community equipment providers offer a critical service, which if not provided safely or effectively, can put the lives and wellbeing of service users at risk. Poor service provision can also have a huge knock-on effect upon wider health and social care related services, e.g. hospital admissions. It is therefore crucial that community equipment providers, including retailers, are very clear about what is expected from them; it is equally important that they are properly resourced and equipped in order to meet the demands and expectations placed upon them.

In addition to operational aspects, providers are expected to abide by many legal, health and safety and medical device management duties and obligations. It is essential that providers are made aware of these and that there is assurance of their ability to comply with these. It is also important when authorities or regions are working to the retail model that, where retailers 'up-sell' products above what has been prescribed, there is clarity around specific roles and responsibilities, particularly in relation to product safety, complaints and liability issues.

The use of third party contractors for some parts of service provision does not remove the legal responsibilities of statutory providers and commissioners. Should parts of community equipment provision be outsourced by the main provider then there is a responsibility on the main provider to ensure legal obligations are met. In the case of retail provision there are still some ambiguous aspects of responsibility but commissioners should make it clear to retailers what they should be complying with.

Note that where services are fully outsourced there is still a full requirement for the outsourced provider to comply with all the Code standards set out below. Outsourcing services does not remove any legal duties or responsibilities.

Refer to Appendix 1 for the full legal and welfare framework relating to the provision of community equipment, including a guide to the main service-specific legislation which providers are expected to operate within.

CODE STANDARD 9

Operational Management

OUTCOME

All operational and contract management responsibilities are clearly defined with designated leads.

Introduction to Code standard 9

In a community equipment store operational management responsibilities are very broad and cover almost all aspects of service delivery. Most services will have a single operational manager, or contracts manager (particularly for outsourced services), in place, with ultimate responsibility for ensuring all aspects of operational management are achieved. There may also be other managers in place with particular responsibilities, e.g. technical manager, but this will very much depend on the size and scope of the service.

Some areas where equipment is provided will not have dedicated storage facilities, e.g. providers of continuing healthcare equipment, equipment issued in special schools. Where this is the case the provider will still work to many of the topic headings identified below.

Generally the issues below will not apply to retailers; however certain aspects will inevitably apply where functions are undertaken on behalf of, or in support of, statutory provision.

9.1 The operational lead, or contract manager, is supported by an operational team and ensures, has knowledge of, and is able to demonstrate how, the following aspects of service delivery are being achieved:

i. **Financial management**

Budget management; pooled funding (where appropriate), invoicing, etc.

ii. **Service management**

Strategy of service; management of projects.

iii. **Performance & information management**

Production of performance statistics; identifying trend lines and projections; issue of data reports.

iv. **Information management**

Management of all information technologies, including setup and scheduling of reports; ensuring information is accurate.

v. **Stock management**

Product management; managing trends; maintaining safety stock levels; ensuring equipment recall systems exist; monitoring and updating IT systems; management of satellite (buffer) stores (where appropriate).

vi. **Store management**

Building management, including all satellite stores; facilities management.

vii. **Staff management**

Staff training; handling staff related issues; ensuring appropriate staffing levels are available; Criminal Record Bureau (CRB) checks.

viii. **Contract management**

Monitoring performance; monitoring third party supplier performance; writing contracts and service level agreements with third party providers.

ix. **Logistics management**

Vehicle and fleet management; managing urgent and out of hour deliveries.

x. **Procurement management**

Facilitating equipment selection processes; carrying out negotiations with suppliers; developing product selection specifications.

xi. **Asset management**

Managing planned maintenance, repair, recycling, refurbishment, scrapping or writing off, and traceability of all assets.

xii. **Health and safety and risk management**

Management of all health and safety and risk issues through formal policies, procedures, assessments, and monitoring arrangements where appropriate. Example areas will include: maintenance of all equipment, medical device management.

xiii. **Clinical services interface**

Meeting clinical need; addressing clinical priorities; prescriber training.

xiv. **Customer service/patient care**

Dealing with customer satisfaction, complaints, and having a formal complaints procedure; having a contact number and individual to handle customer issues.

xv. **Quality management**

Having Total Quality Management (TQM) Systems in place; carrying out regular 'spot checks', and regular audits.

xvi. **Policies & procedures**

Writing & updating policies; implementing new policies; having processes in place for ensuring policies and procedures are being followed.

CODE STANDARD 10

Quality Management Systems

OUTCOME

Quality management systems are built into the service provider's business practice.

Introduction to Code standard 10

Given the nature of community equipment provision, in that services are generally delivered to vulnerable people, it is most important that a good quality service is provided.

Quality is not something that happens of its own accord, it has to be properly managed. There are various approved techniques and standards available for managing quality, e.g. ISO 9000, otherwise known as quality management systems. Quality management is considered to have three main components: *quality control, quality assurance* and *quality improvement*. Quality management is focused not only on product quality, but also the means to achieve it. Quality management therefore uses quality assurance and control of processes as well as products to achieve more consistent quality.

In an environment where community equipment is provided, examples of quality management might be something as simple as having a procedure for testing new products, or a guide for assembling equipment. Quality will be consistent throughout all aspects of the service, ranging from procurement processes to decontamination and storage standards.

Quality management principles should apply in all areas where community equipment is provided, e.g. special schools, stores, retailers.

10.1 Community equipment providers are working to a robust quality management system which covers all operational aspects of service delivery. Services are working to a recognised British, European, Harmonised (e.g. BS/EN), or ideally, International Standard (e.g. ISO 9000), or equivalent. The requirements that a good quality management system will aim to cover include, but are not limited to:

- a set of procedures that cover all key processes, e.g. operational policy
- monitoring of processes to ensure they are effective
- keeping adequate records
- checking output for defects, with appropriate and corrective action where necessary
- regularly reviewing individual processes and the quality system itself for effectiveness
- facilitating continual improvement.

10.2 There are documented and up to date policies and procedures in place, accessible to all staff members, covering all operational functions of the service.

10.3 All staff working within the provider service are fully aware of, and are working to the relevant section of, the policies and procedures applicable to their role.

CODE STANDARD 11

Training and Qualifications
OUTCOME
Staff are appropriately trained in relation to the tasks they are required to undertake.

Introduction to Code standard 11
Training is an area often overlooked where the provision of community equipment is concerned. Training needs to be viewed as broadly as possible, covering all aspects of service provision, e.g. stores management, technical skills, etc. The MHRA[13] has emphasized the importance of appropriate training in its 'Managing Medical Devices'[14] guidance, and has detailed the considerations to be given for each role. The guidance states that all aspects of training in relation to service provision should be incorporated into a policy, or procedures, document.

Where functions of community equipment provision are outsourced to third party providers it is equally important to ensure their staff are suitably trained and qualified to undertake their duties.

Training issues are also important where the TCES Retail Model is adopted; in particular, training should be considered in relation to demonstration, fitting and installation of equipment. Retailers can offer a wider range of choice other than the standard catalogue items, and are able to market to self-funders by up-selling products to service users. These issues need to be given careful consideration. It cannot be assumed that retailer staff have the adequate skills, and a requirement for their training must be made.

---

[13] Medicines and Healthcare products Regulatory Agency.
[14] MHRA (2006). *Managing Medical Devices. Guidance for healthcare and social services organisations.* DB2006(05) only available on website: www.mhra.gov.uk

Training, in the provision of community equipment, needs to be viewed from three different perspectives:

   i.   management of community equipment provision
   ii.   technical skills
   iii.   professional users (qualifications and training for professional staff are dealt with in more detail in Part 3).

11.1 All training related policies and procedures are incorporated into a Policy Document, accessible to all members of staff.

11.2 All staff responsible for the day to day management of equipment provision are appropriately trained and qualified with specific emphasis upon their specialized area of work. Service providers have specified to retailers that their staff have to be adequately trained.

11.3 Depending on their role in community equipment provision all staff are suitably trained and qualified in some or all of the following subjects:

- policy & procedures – local, corporate and national
- health, safety and legislation
- health and safety management (for management)
- performance and contract management
- stores and stock management
- technical & maintenance management
- community equipment IT systems – store, clinical and information
- financial management, including pooled funding arrangements
- customer care (relevant where there is service user interface, e.g. retail provision).

11.4 Staff employed to undertake repair and maintenance responsibilities are suitably qualified to do so, depending upon the level of technical work required. As a general guide the MHRA suggests that for simple devices NVQ level 2[15], or equivalent, is appropriate, and for technically complex equipment NVQ level 3, or equivalent, is required. Where appropriate,

---

[15] NVQs are being replaced by new qualifications under the Qualifications and Credit Framework (QCF). NVQs are expected to remain valid until August 2012.

there are training contracts in place with suppliers/manufacturers to train on technically complex equipment and new technologies.

Note. The organisation SEMTA[16] has developed occupational standards specifically for community equipment technicians, both levels 2 and 3. Examples of some duties carried out at the different levels as set out by SEMTA can be viewed as supporting guidance in Appendix 3.

11.5 Where applicable, staff coming into contact with the public are trained in appropriate communication methods, including communication tactics with deaf and hard of hearing people, for example. Where appropriate, consideration for language will be required.

11.6 Where staff come into direct contact with service users, they are provided with appropriate awareness training, looking at the qualities needed to work with people with disabilities.

11.7 Training is provided by accredited or approved trainers.

11.8 On-going and refresher training is available to reflect the developments in the range of equipment and changes in technical specification.

CODE STANDARD 12

Information Technology and Information Management
OUTCOME
Information is available in a suitable format, is meaningful, and is communicated appropriately and in a timely manner.

Introduction to Code standard 12
There is a clear correlation between good quality information and equipment services which have invested in specialist IT systems. The success of community equipment provision, from an overall performance perspective, is partly

---

[16] 'SEMTA' is the Sector Skills Council for science, engineering and manufacturing technologies in the UK.

dependent upon the robustness and quality of the data provided by the community equipment provider's IT system.

It is also important to ensure that those operating the IT systems understand their functionalities. To ensure information and data are accurate, and that high standards of accuracy are maintained, it is essential that regular data quality checks are in place, and also that appropriate initial and on-going training is provided by competent trainers to the users of the IT systems.

IT systems are also crucial for collecting some referral and clinical information. They can also provide a virtual authorisation check, and can offer virtual budget management solutions for clinical budget holders.

Where the TCES Retail Model has been adopted there will be different reporting mechanisms, especially as equipment and activities will be coming from a variety of sources.

To ensure pooled funding and joint working arrangements continue to work well it is important to ensure that adequate information is supplied by retailers' and is in a meaningful format. Having an interface between retailers systems and in-house performance systems might be something worth exploring.

12.1 IT systems used by community equipment providers are 'fit for purpose', meeting all clinical, financial and operational functionality requirements, whilst adhering to local and national data protection issues.

12.2 There is evidence of audit and governance ('policing') arrangements in place to ensure the information provided by third party sources to the IT system is correct, and also that the data provided is being input correctly; this is supported by policy. Audit and data quality checks take place on a cyclical basis.

12.3 IT systems used for the provision of community equipment have the ability to identify the location of equipment in the event of a recall. This is especially important in regions which have opted for retail provision.

12.4 Training on the use of IT systems used for providing community equipment is delivered by someone competent to do so.

12.5 Training is provided to all members of staff using the system, and peripheral technologies, e.g. handheld devices. This includes: management; stores operatives; administrators; technicians; drivers; prescribers.

12.6 Appropriate certification with renewal dates is issued with initial training, supported by an up to date database of active users.

Refer to Appendix 4 for supporting guidance and examples of the different subject areas individuals should be trained on in relation to their job roles, when using IT systems for the provision of community equipment.

12.7 To ensure data security, all staff members appropriately trained on the use of the community equipment IT system are issued with a secure personal identification number (PIN), or some form of approved User ID. A central database is used to hold details of 'live' users of the system, and also to keep track of changes. There is also an information sharing protocol in place and accessible to all system users. This is in keeping with organisational Data Protection and information sharing obligations.

12.8 Data cleansing policies and procedures are in use. This includes a continual update function for deceased service users.

CODE STANDARD 13

Health and Safety Management

OUTCOME

The health and safety of service users and staff is promoted at all times, supported by clear policy, procedure and guidance.

Introduction to Code standard 13

Health and safety is a very broad topic area, spreading into all aspects of service provision. It is most important that all relevant health and safety issues are addressed in all aspects of community equipment provision, e.g.

commissioning, assessment and service provision, including retail elements. The potential for exposure to serious risk (e.g. electrocution, cross contamination) is inherent with community equipment; in view of this, health and safety management should play a prominent role in the day to day running of community equipment services.

Most of the relevant health and safety requirements relating to community equipment are covered under the Health and Safety at Work Act etc. 1974 (HASAWA). The main aims of the HASAWA are to impose on an employer a statutory duty of care for the health, safety and welfare of its employees, and other people who may be affected by its activities (e.g. service users, the employees of contractors or members of the public).

Failure to comply with the HASAWA – whilst factoring in reasonable practicability – could result in prosecution. Serious breaches of health and safety requirements also carry the penalty of imprisonment for employees held responsible, under the Health and Safety (Offences) Act 2008.

Note that HASAWA covers all aspects of work including computer use and working conditions, etc. However this Code of Practice is only concerned with areas specific to the provision of community equipment.

Where the TCES Retail Model has been adopted it is most important to ensure responsibilities are clearly defined. If they are not clear, issues may arise relating to implied terms, passage and title of risk, product liability and general product safety regulations, for example. Failure to address these issues may result in breaches of various pieces of legislation, e.g. Consumer Protection Act 1987 and the HASAWA.

13.1 There is a Health and Safety policy document covering at least the following areas:

- contracting arrangements
- risk management processes – including monitoring and reviewing (Management of Health and Safety at Work Regulations 1999)
- compliance with medical device issues
- the Provision and Use of Work Equipment Regulations (PUWER) 1998
- the Lifting Operations and Lifting Equipment Regulations (LOLER) 1998

- the Reporting of Injuries, Diseases and Dangerous Occurrences Regulations 1995 (RIDDOR)
- competent health and safety advice.

13.2 The community equipment provider can demonstrate compliance with HASAWA requirements relating specifically to community equipment. Evidence of compliance with the Health and Safety Executive recommended POPMAR process, or similar approach, would be acceptable for ensuring good health and safety principles are embedded into the service.

Basically the POPMAR process involves:
- **P**olicy setting
- **O**rganizing staff
- **P**lanning and setting standards
- **M**easuring performance
- **A**uditing and **R**eviewing

Refer to Appendix 6 for a fuller explanation of the POPMAR model, as recommended by the Health and Safety Executive.

13.3 All provider employees are responsible for recognising when an incident, or a near miss, has occurred, and they have a formal procedure to follow which enables them to report adverse incidents in a timely and appropriate manner.

13.4 Risk assessments are carried out as a result of any untoward incidents, and actions taken to prevent recurrence are implemented and documented on the adverse incident reports.

13.5 There is documentation clearly setting out roles and responsibilities relating to general product safety; this includes all retailers providing community equipment on behalf of statutory organisations.

CODE STANDARD 14

Transportation

OUTCOME

All equipment is safely transported.

Introduction to Code standard 14

The safe transportation of community equipment is very important, as it poses risks to the driver and to the end user. There is also the possibility of damaging the equipment while in transit. Issues arise in particular where clean and potentially contaminated equipment are regularly transported together to and from people's homes. The Carriage of Dangerous Goods by Road Regulations 1996 place strict control on many aspects of transporting arrangements, e.g. the packaging and handling of contaminated equipment; the segregation of clean and contaminated equipment; securing of loads and safe methods of transportation.

The TCES Retail Model brings with it some challenges in relation to transportation as the retailers will be expected to use suitable vehicles for delivering equipment. The Retail Model also expects some service users to collect their prescribed equipment in their personal vehicle. Consideration will have to be given to these issues, as they could present significant risks to the service user.

14.1 Staff transporting equipment in their personal vehicles only do so when it is safe, without risk of cross contamination or injury to themselves or others, and is covered formally by a suitable individual or corporate insurance policy. It may be necessary to have harnessing bolts installed in the vehicles or alternative suitable means for securing equipment, e.g. straps or a separate boot. A policy for staff transporting equipment in personal vehicles is available which includes risk assessment.

14.2 Commissioners or providers have appropriate delivery mechanisms in place to ensure service users or members of the public are not unreasonably expected to collect or transport their own equipment, as this may be deemed to be infringing The Carriage of Dangerous Goods by Road

Regulations 1996. Exceptional circumstances may apply for small aids, but the criteria for this are clearly set out in a procedure document, and communicated to the service user, where appropriate.

14.3 There is a local policy for the management and transport of community equipment from the point of use to the decontamination facility; this may be part of a wider organisational transport policy.

14.4 Vehicles used for transporting contaminated equipment are made of suitable material which allows the vehicle to be satisfactorily cleaned.

14.5 Vehicles used for transporting both clean and contaminated equipment have appropriate segregation controls in use, which also comply with local infection control policy.

14.6 Vehicles used for transporting equipment are of an appropriate size and shape to accommodate the various equipment types, e.g. beds and hoists, and have appropriate adaptations, e.g. ramps, lifts, where appropriate, to carry equipment.

14.7 Vehicles used for transporting equipment are suitably equipped with gloves, aprons, bags for contaminated equipment, and cleaning agents for hands, etc.

14.8 Appropriate hazard warning signs are displayed on vehicles.

14.9 Where service users are expected to collect and transport their own equipment they are advised of the risks and are given written instructions on the best methods for transporting equipment.

CODE STANDARD 15

Decontamination

OUTCOME

Users and staff are kept safe and free from contamination or infection by ensuring decontamination of all medical devices, facilities and vehicles is properly managed.

Introduction to Code standard 15

Where community equipment is loaned to service users and brought back in for reuse when no longer needed, the potential for cross infection is one of the greatest service user safety concerns. Compliance with MHRA Medical Device guidance should be followed to ensure risks of contamination and cross-infection are minimised. It is very important to ensure all equipment is decontaminated before being re-issued to another service user.

15.1 Providers ensure the safety of service users, carers and staff by having appropriate systems in place, so that all reusable medical devices are properly decontaminated prior to use or repair, and that the risks associated with decontamination facilities and processes are well managed.

15.2 The assumption is made that all reused medical equipment is contaminated and staff have precautions in place to reduce the risk to themselves and others, e.g. safe systems of work, personal and suitable protective equipment and/or clothing.

15.3 Medical devices are decontaminated and stored in accordance with legislative and best practice requirements, e.g. manufacturer's guidance, MHRA guidance.

15.4 Dedicated and suitable facilities are used for decontaminating equipment. These facilities are of a suitable size in proportion to the activity requirements and throughput. They are easily accessible, with complete segregation from clean equipment.

15.5 Local protocols are in place to consider decontamination requirements before reusable medical devices are acquired to ensure they are compatible with the decontamination equipment available. Examples of those to be included in the protocol for consultation, or for generally seeking advice, include:

- manufacturer of device
- manufacturer of decontamination/reprocessing equipment
- infection control staff
- consultant microbiologist or consultant in communicable disease
- competent health and safety advisers
- device and equipment users
- advice from MHRA
- in-house technical/decontamination staff
- clinical professionals.

15.6 There are different methods of decontamination used to address varying levels of contamination, depending on the device, risk assessment classification and its use. The methods of decontamination could include: cleaning, cleaning followed by disinfection and/or sterilization. Community equipment providers have in place a protocol which describes the type of equipment and suitable decontamination processes.

Refer to supporting guidance in Appendix 7 relating to classification of infection risk together with the recommendations for appropriate decontamination treatments.

15.7 Where third party contractors carry out cleaning on behalf of community equipment providers a detailed service specification covering all aspects of decontamination is in place. Equipment returned from third party contractors is labelled with a certificate, or clearly marked, to demonstrate it has been appropriately decontaminated.

15.8 Regardless of where equipment has been in the system, e.g. subject to inspection, maintenance, or repair, either on site or at the manufacturer's premises, it is decontaminated before being returned to stock available for issue. Equipment is decontaminated prior to being scrapped.

15.9 Any loaned equipment, or equipment on trial being returned to a manufacturer or supplier, is decontaminated with appropriate certification attached.

15.10 When equipment has been appropriately decontaminated it is labelled, or clearly marked, accordingly and, where appropriate, a declaration of contamination status form is completed. This is readily accessible to the recipient of the equipment. Electronic tracking information also highlights the decontamination status of each piece of equipment.

15.11 Chemicals used are compatible with the device and at the correct concentration as recommended by the various manufacturers involved.

15.12 The decontamination equipment used to clean community equipment is properly commissioned and validated. It is also subject to planned maintenance by properly trained and competent staff. Maintenance records are available for assessment.

15.13 Staff expected to carry out decontamination are:

- appropriately trained
- aware of needle sticks and sharps injury procedures
- provided with suitable equipment/clothing
- made aware of legal requirements
- able to access policies and procedures.

15.14 Should the user or carer be expected to decontaminate equipment, before disposal for example, appropriate information and equipment, e.g. bags and gloves, are provided. This is especially relevant where the TCES Retail Model is used.

15.15 The provider has a senior member of staff and single point of contact to manage and communicate all aspects of decontamination. The decontamination procedures are clearly understood at all levels throughout the provider organisation.

15.16 The provider has clear lines of responsibility for decontamination matters across the organisation, leading to the commissioning board (e.g. Health and Wellbeing Board).

15.17 Senior managers and/or the commissioning board monitor and regularly review decontamination procedures through audit. This is documented and sent to appropriate Medical Device Management Board, and/or appropriate health and safety, or risk, officer for sign-off.

CODE STANDARD 16

Performance Management

OUTCOME

Performance is linked to and can be measured against individual and organisational objectives.

Introduction to Code standard 16

As with any service or contract, it is most important to ensure relevant performance measures are in place to capture the overall performance of service provision. Performance standards will generally be set by those with commissioning responsibilities, although these will also have to be agreed by the provider to ensure the standards are realistic and achievable. Providers may also wish to set their own standards so that they can manage internal performance better, especially where there is dependence upon third party contractors.

It is equally important to ensure that relevant performance related issues are captured for retailer provision, under the TCES Retail Model. It may be useful to have systems and processes in place for monitoring the number of prescriptions issued; how many were redeemed; and when they were redeemed. It will be in the interests of retailers performing well to demonstrate this by providing robust performance management information.

16.1 Providers, including retailers, have robust reporting mechanisms in place in order to satisfy commissioners and internal and external auditors that performance can be assessed and is at an acceptable level.

16.2 Various performance reports are available which cover key areas of the service. Examples of these include, but are not limited to:

- Key Performance Indicators (KPIs) management reports, e.g. number delivered within a certain period
- reasons for failing to deliver equipment within agreed timescale
- waiting lists, or unredeemed prescriptions
- stock value, turnaround, write-offs, collection rates and recycling levels
- number of assets requiring maintenance (planned maintenance schedule) or Portable Appliance Testing (PAT) and Lifting Operations and Lifting Equipment Regulations 1998 (LOLER). This may include urgent repair targets
- third party supplier performance (e.g. lead times)
- savings achieved
- cost saving strategies through improved recall systems, recycling and improved maintenance schedule
- health and safety action plan
- findings from risk assessments
- number of accolades and complaints
- number of near misses/incidents/investigations
- service user satisfaction surveys
- staff turnover levels
- infection control (random spot checks)
- quality controls processes in place, e.g. policies and procedures.

CODE STANDARD 17

Emergency and Out of Hour Cover

OUTCOME

Service users or their carers will at all times have access to emergency repairs or replacement of equipment.

Introduction to Code standard 17

Some community equipment is highly technical and requires regular maintenance. Occasionally equipment needs to be repaired, or in some cases replaced. It is important that service users are able to obtain a repair or replacement for certain types of equipment at any time, even out of hours or on a public holiday, particularly if the service user or their carer is completely dependent upon the equipment (e.g. hoist), as without it they or their carer's health and wellbeing could be at risk.

It is obviously not viable for providers to be available at any time of the day or night, 7 days a week, all year. It is however possible to ensure that service users have at least a contact number where concerns can be discussed and dealt with as appropriate.

17.1 Where appropriate the provider has emergency cover in place at all times for service users in the event of equipment breakdown, to include: normal working hours; outside normal working hours; weekends, and public holidays.

17.2 Where appropriate, cover is in the form of repair, (either in the service user's home or at the provider's premises), or replacement of the equipment, where practicable. Where repair or replacement is not an immediate option, procedures are in place to ensure the service user and/or their carer is made safe until the equipment can be repaired properly or replaced.

17.3 Service users are provided with contact details and instructions should problems arise with their equipment; this includes an out of hours telephone helpline number, and a troubleshooting checklist for their equipment, if appropriate.

It is understood that the above arrangements will not be applicable for every piece of equipment, but evidence should be available which demonstrates that appropriate risk assessments have been undertaken to identify which pieces of equipment will have emergency cover available out of hours. Note this should also factor in such things as the service user's independence, e.g. will the service user be able to get out of bed? It is also important to note that repairs and replacements are only made when the need of the service user is unchanged – i.e. the product is still appropriate to the service user's needs.

CODE STANDARD 18

Stock Management

OUTCOME

Stock is managed efficiently whilst ensuring optimum output is achieved.

Introduction to Code standard 18

Having appropriate levels of stock in place is crucial for community equipment provision, especially where being out of stock could result in, for example, someone being admitted to hospital. It is important for services to ensure that arrangements are in place to include back-up systems detailing alternative products in the event that certain product lines are not in stock. Holding adequate stock does however have to be balanced with acquisition and stock holding costs. Obviously stocking issues are only relevant to products that are normally considered to be 'stock' items.

Holding adequate stock levels is also important for retailers to ensure that they can fulfil prescription orders. Failure to keep adequate levels of prescription items in stock could result in inconvenience for service users, wasted travel time and cost, and delay in receiving equipment. It could also force clients to top-up unnecessarily.

18.1 There is a robust (ideally electronic) stock control system in place, with a designated lead responsible for managing stock levels.

18.2 Appropriate safety stock levels are in place within stores, and at retail outlets, for ensuring the likelihood of running out of stock is minimised, with suitable back-up systems in place providing alternative (clinically approved) products, where certain product lines are not in stock.

18.3 Regular cyclical stock audits are in place with reconciliation updates on the stock management system, where necessary. The procedure for dealing with shortfalls is written into an appropriate 'Writing Off' or 'Disposal' policy.

18.4 Retailers have been provided with a list of products they are normally expected to hold as stock items.

CODE STANDARD 19

Recycling

OUTCOME

Equipment lifespan and levels of recycling[17] are maximised through efficient collection procedures, appropriate servicing, maintenance, decontamination and refurbishing of equipment.

Introduction to Code standard 19

Recycling equipment is a fundamental part of the overall provision of community equipment. As equipment is issued on loan, inevitably equipment will come back into the service for reuse. An efficient service will maximise recycling levels in preference to purchasing new equipment as this can represent a significant cost saving. This is particularly important for complex and specialist equipment which not only is generally difficult to acquire, but it also usually very expensive. It is also important that any equipment recycled for reuse is of an acceptable standard from both a health and safety and medical device management perspective.

The TCES Retail Model is set up to provide simple aids to daily living and does not generally encourage recycling for these products. However, those organisations applying the Retail Model will usually still need to have recycling facilities for equipment not covered by the Retail Model.

---

[17] Recycling incorporates the retrieval, cleaning and decontamination, maintenance, repair and refurbishment, so that equipment is fit for reissue.

19.1 Community equipment providers ensure that returned equipment is cleaned and refurbished to a standard which meets manufacturers, health and safety, MHRA[18], and infection control requirements, before being re-issued. Consideration is also given to the method of suitable repackaging, where appropriate.

19.2 A recycling policy is in place for ensuring a quality, cost effective service for the servicing, maintenance, decontaminating and refurbishing of equipment in order that the equipment lifespan is optimised, accounting for both the number of cycles of use and maximum number of years in use. The policy should cover, but should not necessarily be limited to:

- recycling instructions
- recycling performance levels
- collection performance levels
- scrapping and 'writing off' policy
- salvaging equipment for parts
- guidance on repair, refurbishment and modifications.

CODE STANDARD 20

Assembling, Fitting and Demonstrating Equipment

OUTCOME

Equipment is safely assembled, fitted and demonstrated by suitably trained and qualified staff.

Introduction to Code standard 20

The range of community equipment is vast, and comes in all shapes and sizes. Equipment also comes with different levels of complexity in terms of assembly, fitting and demonstration requirements. For example there is not a great deal of technical input required when delivering a walking frame. On the other hand a

---

[18] Note MHRA have developed all the necessary information required for decontaminating community equipment: MHRA (2006). *Managing Medical Devices. Guidance for healthcare and social services organisations.* DB2006(05) only available on website: www.mhra.gov.uk. MHRA (2003). *Community Equipment Loan Stores – Guidance on Decontamination,* DB2003(06).

profiling bed with a high risk pressure mattress requires very careful assembly, fitting and demonstration.

Equipment poorly assembled and fitted can be very dangerous, and there are cases where this has resulted in serious incidents and fatalities. This aspect of service delivery should be given due care and attention, when considering roles, responsibilities, competencies and training requirements. This section is also directly relevant where the TCES Retail Model is adopted as some retailers are expected to assemble, fit and demonstrate equipment.

Please note this particular section does not apply to minor adaptations. These are specifically addressed within Code standard 21.

20.1 All staff delivering equipment which requires assembling and fitting are suitably trained and qualified to do so. Training received is appropriate to the complexity of the equipment to be assembled and fitted.

20.2 Written procedures are in place outlining the correct processes to be followed for installation, fitting and demonstrating equipment. These include, but are not limited to:

- equipment types, and the different levels of training and qualifications required
- use of manufacturers' and/or in-house written instructions for users
- warnings and safety notices
- building structure and load bearing considerations
- demonstration for the service user and/or carer, including: verbal explanations, the correct use of the equipment in-situ, responding to any questions, queries, or concerns raised by the service user.

20.3 Equipment is installed, fitted and/or adjusted, in accordance with the manufacturer's instructions, and complies with specifications supplied by the clinical prescriber.

20.4 At each delivery the service provider unpacks the equipment, safely removing all wrapping and packaging, and leaves any specific manufacturers', or otherwise approved, instructions for the prescriber, carer, or service user, as appropriate.

20.5 Where necessary, staff have the appropriate communication skills and training to enable them to advise customers, service users and carers on safe use of equipment. This training should include communication tactics with deaf and hard of hearing people.

20.6 Where appropriate, service users, carers and families are part of any dialogue relating to the installation, fitting and/or adjusting of the equipment. This may form part of a risk assessment which outlines the capacity of the individual or carer to understand the training/demonstration and the potential need to offer written advice and review of training. Notification that training has been received is documented by the trainer and, where appropriate, put on the service user's patient record.

CODE STANDARD 21

Minor Adaptations

OUTCOME
Adaptations are made, and equipment safely installed, by suitably trained and qualified staff.

Introduction to Code standard 21
Minor adaptations generally refer to minor alterations made to a service user's property. Adaptations are for the purpose of increasing or maintaining functional independence to enable the service user to remain in their own home, to ensure safety and/or to assist carers by minimising the physical demands placed on them.

The main areas where adaptations may be necessary include, but are not limited to:

- moving and handling, e.g. ceiling track hoists
- household and environmental fittings, e.g. curtain and window openers
- access, e.g. grab rails, portable ramps, door fitments

- personal hygiene, e.g. showers.

Community equipment stores will usually have, or work in conjunction with, technicians. These technicians will be trained in the process for installing minor adaptations, and similar duties. Some retailers are taking on the role of installing simple aids to daily living, e.g. grab rails, toilet surrounds. It is very important therefore that where these duties are undertaken, on behalf of statutory bodies, by the retailers, a risk assessment has been undertaken and that the retailer has been provided with the appropriate skills and training required for undertaking the task.

21.1 Organisations, both commissioners and providers, have clear guidance, including eligibility criteria, about service user's entitlement to home adaptations. This is in line with Local Authorities' Fair Access to Care Services guidance.

21.2 Provision of adaptations only takes place following an individual assessment of need by an Occupational Therapist, Occupational Therapy Assistant or other suitably qualified Therapist or Technician.

21.3 Where an adaptation is required, a process seeking formal agreement is followed. This may include the service user, carer, other members of the household, and other appropriate agencies.

21.4 There are formal checks in place to ensure those undertaking home adaptations are suitably qualified to do so; this applies to internal and external (third party) providers, including retailers. See Code standard 11, Training and Qualifications, for recommended competency levels.

21.5 Where appropriate, service users, carers and families are part of any dialogue relating to the installation, fitting and/or adjusting of the equipment.

21.6 Following the installation of an adaptation, appropriate quality checks are made to ensure all fitness for purpose, quality and safety requirements have been fully met. Checks are carried out by someone suitably qualified to do so, e.g. it might be acceptable for an Occupational Therapist/Technician to check a grab rail, but it may require an individual suitably qualified in Engineering/Building Control, to assess a Ceiling Track Hoist, for example. Quality checks are accompanied by a certificate of compliance, or equivalent. Healthcare professionals involved in the care of the service user have access to records to see when maintenance checks were last carried out and with what result. Guidance outlining the above requirements should be clearly documented.

CODE STANDARD 22

Manual Handling

OUTCOME

Manual handling processes are in place to ensure risks are minimised and safety is a priority for staff, carers and service users.

Introduction to Code standard 22

The provision of community equipment often involves a series of manual handling tasks. For example, equipment will need to be manually handled within a store, or when staff deliver, install, or maintain equipment. This may also involve heavy equipment being manually handled upstairs in service users' homes, e.g. beds, hoists. Equipment is also regularly manually handled by service users, e.g. when collecting from retailers, or carers within and around the home.

As Manual Handling Operations Regulations 1992 apply to all stakeholders and providers of the service, individual partners, service providers (including third party contractors), and employees (including clinical professionals), all are responsible for ensuring manual handling risks are minimised and, where possible, avoided, which could otherwise result in injury.

22.1 Safe handling procedures are in place to ensure manual handling risks are minimised and safety is a priority for staff and service users.

22.2 Measures are in place to avoid the risk of injury from manual handling so far as is reasonably practicable.

22.3 Where manual handling cannot be avoided, a suitable and sufficient risk assessment is carried out, including the task, load, working environment, physical capabilities of the staff and service users involved, and any other relevant factors.

22.4 Any manual handling risks to service users, staff and carers associated with moving and installation of the equipment itself are considered, e.g. service users or carers collecting equipment from retailers in personal vehicles.

22.5 Where equipment is provided to reduce the risks involved in manual handling (e.g. hoists, slings, electric profiling beds), adequate training, information and instructions on the use of the equipment are provided; this is documented and signed as complete by the service user or their representative.

CODE STANDARD 23

Medical Device Management

OUTCOME

Risks to service users and others through use of equipment are minimised.

Introduction to Code standard 23

Good medical device management is a fundamental part of providing community equipment safely. Failure to ensure medical devices are managed appropriately has resulted in many adverse incidents and even fatalities over recent years. It is essential that medical device management is followed wherever community equipment is provided.

Where organisations have adopted the TCES Retail Model it is important to ensure that medical device issues are covered. It is also important to ensure that responsibilities are clear between commissioners, stores and retailers, as it is easy to assume that someone else is responsible for taking care of certain aspects of medical device management.

One way of clearing any ambiguity around responsibilities is by including medical device responsibilities within any accreditation process. The British Healthcare Trades Association (BHTA) and the National Association of Equipment Providers (NAEP) have jointly developed a very useful 'Community Equipment Dispenser Scheme[19]' to cover the retail aspect of provision, and joining this scheme should be considered to ensure medical device issues are covered by the retailer.

In addition NHS Training for Innovation, originally established by Lord Darzi, has developed Medical Device Training Criteria (particularly for a hospital setting)[20]. This is also a useful source of information to refer to when defining responsibilities.

23.1 Organisations, including commissioners and providers, have the following list, or similar subject headings, covered in policy documentation, and operating procedures, specifically relating to medical device management:

- policies and procedures
- reporting incidents
- Medical Device Management Board (e.g. responsibilities)
- acquisition processes
- electrical safety testing (portable appliance testing)
- repair and maintenance (Lifting Operations and Lifting Equipment Regulations – LOLER, Provision and Use of Work Equipment Regulations 1998 – PUWER, s.3 of the Health and Safety at Work Act 1974 and r.3 of the Management of Health and Safety at Work Regulations 1999)
- training for professional and end users
- information and record management, e.g. user instructions
- decontamination and disposal processes.

Retailers should also be working to similar, albeit less comprehensive, medical device operating procedures.

---

[19] For further details visit: www.cedonline.org.uk
[20] For further details visit: www.tfi.nhs.uk

Note. Refer to Supporting Criteria in Appendix 5 when considering the above headings.

23.2 There are clear lines of accountability throughout the provider organisation, supported by procedures, leading to the commissioning board, including the process for managing medical device alerts.

23.3 The community equipment provider has a designated individual with ultimate responsibility for ensuring what is requested by the Medical Device Management Board within the commissioning organisation, is being delivered. This individual is also responsible for highlighting to the Medical Device Management Board any problems that arise with equipment.

23.4 There are performance and quality reports available to support medical device management, with a particular emphasis upon planned preventative maintenance.

Part 3: Clinical and Professional Responsibilities

Introduction to Code standards 24 to 35

Community equipment is prescribed by almost every clinical professional responsible for delivering care in the community. Clinical professionals generally work with community equipment services and special schools to assist them in providing, for example, therapeutic, mobility, communication, educational, environmental, independence and rehabilitation equipment.

Some examples of the services, functions and equipment provided, to support clinical professionals in their role, include:

- home nursing, e.g. pressure relieving mattresses
- aids for daily living, e.g. shower chairs, kettle tippers
- children's equipment, e.g. postural support chairs
- sensory impairment equipment, e.g. flashing doorbells
- minor adaptations, e.g. ramps, grab rails
- wheelchairs (short term)
- communication aids
- telecare, e.g. environmental aids.

Traditional methods of providing community equipment are changing in some regions with the introduction of retail provision. This is known as the Transforming Community Equipment Services (TCES) Retail Model. Under this model, the traditional assessment process remains unchanged in that clinical professionals such as nurses and therapists assess clients and identify their equipment needs. Unlike traditional provision, under the Model the clinician will issue a prescription for the equipment required, which the client or a representative can redeem at specified retailers.

The client may either redeem the prescription for the 'standard' item at no cost, or may 'top-up' to a superior product and pay the price difference themselves. Retailers are expected to be able to offer advice on suitable alternative products if the client wishes to 'top-up'. Retailers must also be able to supply advice on use and fitting of equipment, both standard and 'top-up' items.

Retailers operating under the Retail Model are consequently taking on in effect some professional responsibilities, in that they are supplying advice on what equipment is suitable for a client's needs, and on how it is to be used.

This Part addresses the standards clinical professionals should be working to when accessing and prescribing community equipment. Although the Part largely relates to therapists and nursing staff, because the TCES Retail Model requires retailers to carry out some activities normally provided by clinical professionals, some sections of this Part relate to retailers where they take on aspects of a clinical role.

This section is not intended to replace, recreate or conflict with any professional standards clinical practitioners are currently working to as part of their professional code of conduct, e.g. Health Professions Council (HPC) – *Standards of proficiency, conduct, performance and ethics*; **Nursing and Midwifery Council (NMC) -** *Standards of conduct, performance and ethics for nurses and midwives.*

When clinical professionals assess for and prescribe community equipment they are expected to adhere to various governing standards and regulations. For example, besides having to meet the standards of their respective councils, they are required to work within organisational and regulatory boundaries. They are also expected to work in co-ordination with the providers of community equipment services. With these issues in mind this Part carefully pulls together the various obligations of clinical professionals, with regard to community equipment.

It is important to note that this Part in no way suggests that the clinical professional is accountable to the community equipment provider for the clinical aspects of their role. However there does need to be collaboration between the two parties where it directly relates to equipment, to ensure a safe and seamless service is provided to the service user.

CODE STANDARD 24

Assessing the Service User's Equipment Needs

OUTCOME

There is a clear, comprehensive, easy to follow, and consistent service user assessment procedure in place which enables all service users' community equipment needs to be identified satisfactorily.

Introduction to Code standard 24

This section is concerned with the service user assessment process, in relation to the provision of community equipment, so that the needs of the service user can best be met. The assessment process is generally straightforward when there is the requirement for a single basic piece of equipment, e.g. walking frame, and where there is only one assessment to meet a certain need. Complications can ensue however when for example a service user has multiple needs, and especially where some of their requirements are for complex equipment, e.g. major adaptations to the home. These difficulties can be compounded where, for example, several clinicians carry out different assessments to meet different health, social care and education needs. Regardless of the service users' needs, it is important to ensure there is an all-embracing and consistent process applied when assessing the service user, to ensure their needs can best be met.

24.1 There is a simple and structured (preferably electronic) process in place to receive and collate referral information. This should link to a database of existing service users, so that it is possible to check information already held about the service user, and whether other clinical professionals are involved in the case. There must be a facility for adding new service users, and for existing service users there is the ability to add the referral data.

24.2 Appropriate screening processes are in place, reflecting appropriate levels of seniority for various levels of need. Screening also includes:

- a process for collecting additional information, where necessary, and ensuring any gaps in the referral data are appropriately dealt with and updated
- a process for dealing with self-assessment

- a process for allocating assessors, including urgent need.

24.3 Once the equipment needs have been assessed, outcomes and decisions are discussed with appropriate authorities, and with the service user or carer, and appropriately documented and communicated; this also reflects the necessary levels of authorisation.

24.4 A policy document or procedure clearly sets out the process for accessing and providing:

- standard equipment (including retailers for simple aids)
- non-standard equipment (e.g. beds and hoists)
- complex and specialist equipment (e.g. bariatric and children's equipment)
- minor adaptations
- major adaptations.

The procedure also sets out the process for arranging service delivery for the various types of equipment provision, including in-house and third party providers (e.g. retailers), where appropriate.

24.5 There is a process in place to allow the original assessor to know that the equipment provision is completed (this includes retail prescription equipment). This prompts arrangements for a review to be carried out to check that the equipment meets the needs. Except in special circumstances, the original assessor co-ordinates delivery of various services and ensures everything is satisfactory, to ensure the service user's needs have been fully met.

24.6 Depending on the service user's situation and the sort of equipment/adaptations provided, the assessor sets a review date based on clinical risk assessment, to ensure the equipment is still meeting the service user's needs, e.g. after one year. As a result this could lead to more assessment, more services, removal or replacement of equipment, or closure of the case.

24.7 Assessments for equipment will factor in the whole-life needs of the service user, and not just the clinical need, e.g. can the user or carer use the equipment; can the equipment be used outside; is it safe in situ.

CODE STANDARD 25

Single Assessment (Co-ordinated Approach)

OUTCOME

The process to enable single assessment is easy to follow and is a seamless experience for the user and carer.

Introduction to Code standard 25

The purpose of the single assessment process is to ensure that service users receive appropriate, effective and timely responses to their health, social care or education needs, and that professional resources are used efficiently. It will promote better care services and better outcomes for people with disabilities and older people; prevent duplication of information; and enable effective sharing of information between health and social care professionals.

In pursuit of these aims, the single assessment process should ensure that the scale and depth of assessment is kept in proportion to the service users' needs; agencies and organisations do not duplicate each other's assessments; and professionals contribute to assessments in the most effective and efficient way.

There are key challenges to the development and implementation of single assessment procedures, e.g. communication, sharing information and training. If co-ordinated appropriately, single assessments can facilitate positive changes to practice. This is especially true in cases where the service user has a variety of health, social care and education equipment needs.

The single assessment promotes the more consistent application of eligibility criteria and encourages more creative approaches to both care and service delivery planning. This would be most beneficial where for example a service user is to be discharged from hospital with health and social care equipment needs.

25.1 A policy is in place to demonstrate that service users receive safe, seamless, and co-ordinated care, treatment and support when more than one provider is involved, or when they move between services.

25.2 An inter-agency protocol exists to reflect the approach to be taken where equipment is necessary to meet a combination of health, education and social care needs. This includes any dialogue and communication requirements with the service user and/or carer, and, where appropriate, third sector organisations.

CODE STANDARD 26

Assessing the Home
OUTCOME

Home assessments are carried out thoroughly, in a clear, timely and consistent manner.

Introduction to Code standard 26

Home assessments can be problematic when, for example, hospital based staff discharge service users with equipment into the community without having physically assessed the home. It can also be problematic when community based staff assess the home for suitability without factoring in such things as: other furniture already in the house; specific dimensions, and accessibility of the house or room, e.g. steps or stairs.

26.1 Where home assessments are undertaken by clinical staff, or Trusted Assessors, this includes evaluation of need based on stated equipment criteria, and use of a standardised risk assessment which enables all reasonable eventualities of risk or harm to be minimised, or removed, should there be a requirement to provide equipment. A dialogue will also be necessary, in some instances, with the user and/or carer.

26.2 For types of community equipment where a physical home assessment will always be necessary, e.g. beds, hoists, the process and equipment inclusion types are set out within local discharge policy or similar guidance.

26.3 Assessments of the home consider the whole-life needs of the service user and not just the clinical needs, e.g. can the equipment be used in certain rooms or can the equipment be used outside, or how does the equipment impact upon other members of the family. Home assessments also have input from the user and/or carer.

26.4 Retailers have been provided with clear instructions relating to findings from home assessments, or issues which may impact upon delivery and fitting arrangements.

CODE STANDARD 27

Training in Equipment Provision and Use

OUTCOME

All training in equipment provided is carried out by suitably trained individuals, and is supplemented by appropriate written information.

Introduction to Code standard 27

Training on equipment provision and use is an area that can easily be overlooked. It is vital for the clinical professional to understand the functions of equipment and how it is to be best used in order to meet the needs of the service user. This section addresses training for both professional and end users, e.g. carers, of equipment.

Training on equipment provision and use also needs to be considered for organisations working with the TCES Retail Model. There has been some concern relating to the competency and training requirements of retailer staff members when required to undertake some of these clinical responsibilities. This is particularly important where the retailer is expected to advise the service user on a suitable alternative product when the original item prescribed is not in stock, for example. Training requirements are an essential part of any retailer accreditation process.

The TCES Retail Model also reduces the direct interface between the clinical professional and the service user when receiving the equipment. Therefore the role of advising on the use of the equipment will in some instances become the responsibility of the retailer. Training requirements for retailers will also need to be considered as part of training in equipment provision and use.

The Medicines and Healthcare products Regulatory Agency (MHRA) has emphasized the importance of appropriate training in its guidance 'Managing Medical Devices', and has detailed the considerations to be given for each role. It has stated that all aspects of training in relation to service provision should be incorporated into a policy document which should be developed by the medical devices management group – should one exist – see Appendix 5 for further details. Note the MHRA guidance is also relevant to retailers.

27.1 A policy document exists which specifies responsibilities for training, together with procedures to be followed for training on equipment provided, both to clinical professionals, retailers and to service users and/or carers.

27.2 Those responsible for prescribing community equipment are given relevant training by suitable individuals, to ensure that they understand how the manufacturer intends the product to be used and that they can relay to the end user (service user or carer) the intended use and functions of the device in order to use it safely, and maximise its performance. Certain, albeit limited, aspects of this requirement will also now apply to retailer staff where they are advising service users directly about equipment in the place of the clinical professional.

27.3 Those with clinical responsibilities are responsible for ensuring that they are appropriately trained and kept up to date on the specific equipment categories they issue. For example this may be achieved through a Continuing Professional Development programme.

27.4 Appropriate training material and support information, e.g. manufacturer's instructions are made available and communicated to professional and end users as appropriate.

27.5 A structure is in place demonstrating the different levels of equipment that can be ordered and provided by the different grades of clinical professionals; this will usually be based upon complexity of equipment, and financial thresholds. In the case of the retailer there is a list available showing which individuals have been appropriately trained to issue equipment on behalf of statutory service providers.

27.6 To ensure new developments in equipment are accessible to users, a stated process for consideration and authorisation of non-standard equipment or equipment that falls outside the current criteria is in place; this also applies where the TCES Retail Model has been adopted. The stated process has explicit timescales where provision cannot be routinely made, to allow time for users to make alternative and informed choices in relation to other potential options.

27.7 Where necessary, staff, including those at retailers, have the appropriate communication skills and training to enable them to advise customers/users /carers on safe use of equipment. This training should include communication tactics with deaf and hard of hearing people.

CODE STANDARD 28

Transportation of Equipment

OUTCOME

All equipment is safely transported, with minimal risk to clinicians, carers and others.

Introduction to Code standard 28

It should not be expected for clinical staff to regularly deliver and collect community equipment in their personal vehicles. It is recognised however that in some instances clinical staff may need to transport equipment. This does present some risks which should be given careful consideration. The following list sets out some examples of the risks to be considered:

- transportation of clean and contaminated equipment in the same vehicle carries the risk of cross contamination, and consequently infecting service users
- clinical staff may not be fully insured to carry equipment in their personal vehicles
- clinical staff could expose themselves to personal injury.

In some instances retailers deliver equipment to service users. Where this is the case it is important that due regard is given to safe transportation issues.

28.1 Clinical staff are never required to carry contaminated equipment in their personal vehicles. Note this also includes equipment used for assessment purposes.

28.2 Where clinical staff deliver clean equipment in their personal vehicles, this is only done where:

- necessary adjustments have been made to vehicles, e.g. secure fixing points
- individuals are properly insured
- a formal risk assessment has been undertaken.

28.3 All of the above issues are reflected in a policy document. This may form part of a larger transport policy.

28.4 When transporting equipment, manual handling risks are controlled and equipment is properly secured.

CODE STANDARD 29

Equipment Selection Process (New Acquisitions)
OUTCOME
There is a clear and consistent process used for selecting equipment which takes into consideration both the organisation's and the service user's needs.

Introduction to Code standard 29

It is absolutely vital that service users receive the right equipment which is best suited to meet their needs. It does not necessarily follow that the 'best' product in the market is the most suitable piece of equipment for the service user. It is also important that whatever equipment is issued, it can be properly supported by the issuing organisation, e.g. ability to maintain the equipment.

It is important therefore to ensure there is a whole-systems approach taken when determining what the best product is to meet the needs of the service user. It is equally important to ensure that the process aligns with local organisational policy, e.g. best value, and that there is sufficient expertise to provide on-going support and maintenance for the equipment.

A fundamental part of medical device management is the acquisition aspect. It is easy to assume that products are safe and of good quality just because they are sold or leased from reputable suppliers. This is not always the case and careful consideration needs to be given to this fundamental issue. Independent advice can be obtained from Disabled Living Centres[21], or the Disabled Living Foundation[22] (DLF), for example.

Under the TCES Retail Model there is a national catalogue in place which authorities can select from and request that their approved retailers provide these items on their behalf. The Department of Health has commissioned an independent company to host and manage a national catalogue and tariff for Simple Aids to Daily Living (SADLs) as an on-going service to Local Authority/NHS TCES teams.

The national catalogue includes the most common items of equipment issued through community equipment stores in England. Generic specifications that meet clinical need have been developed to ensure the widest ranges of equipment items are available in the retail marketplace.

The organisation responsible for hosting the TCES catalogue looks after five aspects of the national catalogue infrastructure:

---

[21] For more information visit: www.assist-uk.org
[22] For more information visit: www.dlf.org.uk

i. maintaining and publishing the generic specifications used for equipment prescriptions in various parts of England
ii. recommending to the Department of Health the redemption value of the prescriptions
iii. a list of specifications prescribed in a particular local area
iv. a list of locally accredited retailers meeting defined standards
v. a list of specific products that meet the specifications at the tariff price and/or with an appropriate top-up charge.

For organisations working with the TCES Retail Model it is recommended to obtain a copy of the equipment selection process from the company hosting the national catalogue. This may be filed and used to demonstrate that there has been a thorough process for selecting equipment types used.

Before using equipment from the agreed TCES Retail Model national catalogue it is important for local areas to ensure that they are satisfied with the equipment selection process which has been used, as this may not comply with internal governance and medical device management policies and procedures.

When equipment types are selected in-house, ideally there should be a formal process to go through when acquiring new equipment, to ensure all safety, quality and suitability issues are addressed. This may be in the form of a product selection group. Having the right representation involved in the equipment selection process is also important, e.g. store managers, technicians, users and clinical professionals, to ensure all views are considered.

It is important to ensure appropriate product or supplier standards are considered when acquiring equipment, e.g. BS/EN harmonised standard, ISO 9001, or the British Healthcare Trades Association (BHTA) Code of Practice[23]. It is also important to ensure formal procurement practice is applied before selecting equipment.

29.1 A policy or procedure is in place to ensure the acquisition of new medical devices addresses safety, quality, and performance issues. This also includes equipment acquired from the TCES national catalogue.

---

[23] BHTA Code of Practice recently attained the Office of Fair Trading Approved Code Logo. A copy of the Code can be located at: www.bhta.net/bhta-code-of-practice.aspx

29.2 Policies include and take account of the needs and preferences of all interested parties, e.g. those involved in use, stores, commissioning, purchasing, decontamination, maintenance and decommissioning, the service user and prescribing clinicians, when selecting equipment.

29.3 Policies align with and support any approved local or national contracts, e.g. TCES national catalogue, or frameworks, in place, as these will usually have undergone a rigorous supplier and product vetting and evaluation process.

29.4 All new acquisitions by clinical professionals are made through appropriate channels, e.g. non-standard processes and products are approved by the product selection group.

29.5 The clinical professionals responsible for selecting and acquiring new equipment have appropriate links with the medical device management board, where one exists.

29.6 Evidence for selecting equipment is based upon the needs of the service user being paramount, whilst factoring in best value.

29.7 There is a procedure in place for any instances where clinical staff operate outside the normal equipment selection process, e.g. when only one product is on the market to meet a specific need.

CODE STANDARD 30

Demonstrating and Trialling Complex, Specialist and Children's Equipment

OUTCOME

Equipment is demonstrated and trialled appropriately and in a safe environment.

Introduction to Code standard 30

Demonstrating community equipment appropriately can be difficult, mainly due to inappropriate facilities, and sometimes lack of resources. Often clinical professionals physically take equipment out in their personal vehicles to service users' homes, or alternatively service users have to visit a store to have equipment demonstrated.

Alternatively some suppliers, particularly for children's equipment, provide demonstrations of equipment at service user's homes. Although this has advantages, particularly for children who feel most comfortable in familiar surroundings, there can be unnecessary delays, particularly if the equipment is not suitable and the service user needs alternative equipment demonstrated, for example. Sometimes equipment can be left with the service user for trialling, as longer periods can be required with certain products to assess suitability, etc. This however is not without problems, e.g. breakdown cover and maintenance responsibilities.

It is important for trials and demonstrations of equipment to take place in the right environment, and in the place where the service user feels most comfortable and is most likely to be using the equipment on a regular basis, e.g. home or school.

30.1 There are appropriate facilities available for service users, carers, and staff to have community equipment suitably and safely demonstrated. There is a policy in place supporting this stating what equipment is available for trial and the various locations this can take place, e.g. an equipment store, home, school.

30.2 Where service users are not able to access the demonstration facilities a suitable appointment is arranged to allow equipment to be appropriately demonstrated and/or trialled.

30.3 Where equipment is either on loan, trial or for assessment purposes, including from a supplier, it is made clear whose responsibility it will be should any problems arise.

CODE STANDARD 31

Community Equipment Related Risk Assessments
OUTCOME
Risks and potential hazards relating to community equipment are identified, prevented or reduced, documented, communicated and managed in a timely and systematic manner.

Introduction to Code standard 31

In a community equipment environment responsibility for assessing and managing risk is shared by different commissioning and provider individuals and organisations, e.g. stores staff, retailers, and clinical professionals. This Code standard is principally taken up with the clinical users of community equipment services, although reference is also made to retailers as those with responsibility for issuing some equipment to service users.

It is important to note that although there are separate clinical and provider responsibilities, there is a requirement for each of these to co-operate on areas where risk factors may overlap, e.g. a clinical professional informing a provider about faulty equipment and the need for a replacement. It is also important to ensure the views of the end user are taken account of, as what is deemed low risk to one service user may indeed be a high risk to another.

Where organisations are working with the TCES Retail Model it is important for clear boundaries to be set in terms of equipment related risks, and risk assessments. For example, if a therapist prescribes a specific type of equipment for the service user and the retailer does not have that type in stock and provides an unsuitable alternative in its place, what are the risks involved and who is responsible for managing them? This is an example of some of the issues to be considered.

Carrying out regular risk assessments is one of the main ways to avoid or minimise the likelihood of incidents occurring, when providing community equipment. There have been a significant number of incidents and even fatalities reported to the Health and Safety Executive (HSE) and Medicines and Healthcare products Regulatory Agency over recent years, specifically relating to community equipment. Section 3 (1) of the Health and Safety at Work etc. Act 1974 states: 'It shall be the duty of every employer to conduct his undertaking in such a way as to ensure, so far as is reasonably practicable, that persons not in his employment who may be affected thereby are not thereby exposed to risks to their health or safety'. This is particularly true for assessing and meeting the equipment needs of service users, as these are deemed to be covered under section 3 of the act as non-employees.

It is also important to consider risk issues in terms of assessing the consequence of not providing the equipment at all. For example failing to provide equipment could result in the service user's condition worsening or in their admission to hospital.

31.1 Risk assessments consider the whole environment where equipment is likely to be used, involve consultation with families and carers, and are carried out in accordance with the requirements of the 'Management of Health and Safety at Work Regulations 1999', including:

- the carrying out of suitable and sufficient risk assessments in respect of both employees and non-employees by a competent person
- making arrangements for the monitoring and reviewing of risk assessments
- putting in place arrangements for the planning, organisation, control, monitoring and review of measures to control risks (preventive and protective measures)
- providing employees with information, instruction and training to ensure their competence and understanding of risks and control measures
- co-operation and co-ordination between different organisations involved in the provision, maintenance and use of the equipment and the delivery of care to individuals.

31.2 The following specific areas are covered by risk assessments, undertaken by clinical users, and retailers (where they make provision on behalf of statutory organisations):

- transportation, assembly and installation of equipment
- safe systems of work and the use of equipment
- risks arising from the home environment
- preventive maintenance and inspection of equipment
- training, information and instruction
- manual handling issues for staff, equipment users and carers
- emergency procedures (e.g. in event of equipment failure or an emergency)
- incident reporting process (where the community equipment provision is hosted by one agency the incident reporting process is communicated across all stakeholders to ensure lessons are learned)
- record keeping
- the interface and overlap with retailers, where applicable.

CODE STANDARD 32

Reviewing Equipment and Equipment Needs
OUTCOME
As long as the service user is in possession of equipment, and has a requirement for it, it is safe, appropriate and continues to meet the service user's needs.

Introduction to Code standard 32
Reviewing equipment and equipment needs does not generally take place as often as it should; in many cases there is just not the resource or capacity available to undertake such a task for every service user. This can present a significant risk to service users should they be issued with equipment without formal follow-up reviews, or reassessment processes in place. For example, a service user may have been provided with a low risk pressure mattress, but over a period of time their condition could deteriorate so that they then require a medium to high risk mattress. Without a formal and regular review, or reassessment process, in place, issues such as this may not be picked up until it is too late.

Equally, without a physical check on the equipment, and possibly a replacement, after a certain period as recommended by the manufacturers, service users could potentially be put at risk by using unsafe equipment.

There is no better person for informing as to whether or not their needs are being met than the service user, as they are using and living with the equipment day in and day out. If the views of the service user are not sought this also could be potentially dangerous.

It goes without saying that some of the simple aids to daily living may not require any follow up, but this should be accordingly risk assessed and be factored into guidance.

It is also important to inform the service user about the expected life of the product by providing the manufacturer's instructions, for example. It would also be useful to request the service user to inform the equipment provider if they feel their needs are not being met by the equipment provided.

32.1 There are guidelines available setting out the review and reassessment of service users' equipment needs. There is a formal and robust process in place for tracking and monitoring review and reassessment dates; ideally this will be electronic.

32.2 There is a systematic, and preferably electronic, process in place for ensuring equipment is reviewed and replaced, where necessary, in accordance with manufacturers' guidance. Information relating to expected equipment life is widely available. Where equipment is provided by a retailer the manufacturer's instructions are issued to the service user.

32.3 There is a process and procedure in place for ensuring the service user can easily relay their concerns in the event that the equipment is no longer meeting their needs. This could include supplying a contact telephone number to report any problems.

32.4 There is an agreed hierarchy of review based on equipment types and clinical risk. This will also factor in such things as maintenance requirements and frequency. Manufacturers and suppliers have input into this process to ensure it is in line with their guidance.

CODE STANDARD 33

Trusted Assessor

OUTCOME

Service user focussed or home assessments are carried out by individuals appropriately qualified to do so.

Introduction to Code standard 33

In view of the mounting pressures placed upon clinical professionals, with more and more services being provided in the community, together with the increasing ageing population, there is often a shortage of professionals available to assess equipment needs. This shortage can result in delays in assessments and equipment provision, and long waiting lists can ensue. In order to combat these issues some areas use support workers to undertake assessments instead of fully qualified therapists and nurses. This approach is to be encouraged as a measure to reduce delays in provision, but should be cautioned by the fact that the support workers may not always have all the necessary skills for this responsible undertaking.

In recognition of the need for support staff to assist in this important role, balanced with the need for staff to be competent in assessing equipment needs, a Trusted Assessor Project[24] has been developed. Principally the project was aimed at providing individuals such as support workers with the necessary skills to ensure service users and their carers get the right equipment in a timely manner. Once the necessary skills are acquired individuals can then call themselves 'Trusted Assessors'. The necessary information to support this project and training has been set out as a 'Competence Framework'.

---

[24] Winchcombe, M. and Ballinger, C (2005). *A Competence Framework for Trusted Assessors*. Manchester: Assist UK, in partnership with: The College of Occupational Therapists; The Chartered Society of Physiotherapy; The Disabled Living Foundation; The Royal National Institute of the Blind; The Royal National Institute for Deaf People.

33.1 Trusted Assessor programmes are only carried out using an approved and accredited trainer and provider.

33.2 Trusted Assessor programmes are linked to approved National Occupational Standards.

33.3 There is formally recognised and approved Trusted Assessor training provided in the assessment, use and fitting of basic daily living equipment.

33.4 A central database exists with up to date training details on all Trusted Assessors, along with other staff who have been identified through performance review to have competencies based on experience to carry out designated assessor duties.

33.5 Regular and on-going training arrangements are in place for Trusted Assessor training in order to keep up to date with changes in service provision.

33.6 All relevant liability issues are addressed where Trusted Assessor training is provided, e.g. professional codes of conduct, local policies and procedures, employment contracts.

CODE STANDARD 34

Self-Assessment

OUTCOME

Where self-assessment practice is encouraged, there is clear guidance around roles, responsibilities and accountabilities.

Introduction to Code standard 34

Where offered, self-assessment is a part of the overall service that enables people to assess their own equipment needs, or to complete an assessment for someone else. Where self-assessment is offered it is important to note that this is not a 'cop-out' in terms of responsibilities. Statutory guidance from the Department of Health points out that a self-assessment is in addition to, but cannot replace or displace, the Local Authority's community care assessment.[25] If anything then, there need to be more rigorous procedures in place, in view of the following:

- the service user may require several pieces of equipment, some of which may be complex, and these may need to be delivered simultaneously
- equipment may require on-going maintenance
- equipment may require replacement every so often according to manufacturer's guidance
- the service user may not be able to collect, install or dispose of equipment due to their disability or illness.

34.1 Where this service is offered proper safeguards and monitoring arrangements are in place to ensure the service user is:

- given the right equipment
- provided with a safe service
- clear about liability and accountability issues
- offered support to complete the necessary forms, where appropriate.

CODE STANDARD 35

Financial and Budgetary Authorisation Processes
OUTCOME
Effective management of resources is ensured through clear financial and budgetary authorisation processes and controls.

Introduction to Code standard 35
Quite often clinical staff will be responsible both for managing equipment budgets for community equipment, and for authorising individual items of expenditure for certain pieces of equipment. Where pooled funding arrangements are in place there may be a 'scheme of delegation' in operation, whereby clinical leads, amongst others, are responsible for managing

[25] Department of Health (2010). *Prioritising need in the context of Putting People First: a whole system approach to eligibility for social care - guidance on eligibility criteria for adult social care, England 2010*, para 84.

equipment expenditure. Sometimes this will be in the form of 'virtual budget management'. Without clear financial and budgetary controls in place for clinical staff, overspends can occur; this in turn can lead to delays in equipment provision.

If clinical staff do not exercise the necessary control when ordering equipment, or if they are not made aware of what existing equipment is available before ordering new, it can have a significant impact upon equipment budgets. It is therefore most important to ensure that the right processes and controls are in place to enable clinical staff to have access to information about the availability of equipment.

Even where clinical staff have no influence over expenditure on equipment it is good practice to ensure they are aware of how much there is available to spend on equipment.

35.1 Where budgetary responsibilities are given to clinical leads, via a scheme of financial delegation or otherwise, clear responsibilities are set out in terms of their budget allocations, and the conditions of expenditure, e.g. thresholds and authorisation levels.

35.2 Clinical leads that have been granted devolved or delegated budget authority are bound by the financial frameworks, e.g. standing orders, and procurement regulations of their employing organisations.

35.3 Budget holders have access to and are able to provide expenditure reports, including committed and projected spend, for example.

35.4 Processes exist to demonstrate how clinical staff ensure the most efficient and best value is achieved when ordering new equipment. For example some community equipment services have employed a clinical team member to monitor all equipment requests, and provide alternatives, where appropriate.

Part 4: Peripheral Issues and Specialist Areas

Introduction to Code standards 36 to 47

Although most equipment is provided via statutory equipment stores, there are a significant number of other sources, e.g. equipment in schools, continuing healthcare equipment. These generally have very few clear boundaries set, in terms of responsibilities and accountabilities for equipment. As a result this type of equipment provision is often overlooked, neglected, and even dangerous. Furthermore, related issues, such as maintenance of equipment provided outside of standard community equipment loan stores, often falls outside of anyone's attention. Quite often these specialist services are only functional because of personal endeavours of committed staff members.

In addition, peripheral aspects of service provision, such as cross border issues and direct payments, can present complications, and can add significant delays to the provision of equipment. Failing to address these issues adequately often exposes service users to lack of clear decision making and subsequently long delays in equipment provision.

Note. Parts 1-3 of this Code of Practice may also have application to organisations providing equipment in a specialist service area (e.g. schools), even if provision is not made through a statutory equipment service. For example, equipment in schools is subject to the same health and safety requirements as a community equipment service, and must be properly commissioned. This Part does not restate relevant requirements already set down in earlier sections; it gives additional requirements relevant specifically to the following specialist areas of provision.

CODE STANDARD 36

Community Equipment in Special Schools
OUTCOME
Equipment is provided safely and meets the individual needs of service users.

Introduction to Code standard 36

The provision of community equipment in special schools is generally considered to be problematic. There are approximately a thousand special schools in England, so this is a cause for real concern. This concern is mainly owing to these schools lacking the appropriate facilities and resources to manage all aspects of service provision, e.g. maintenance and decontamination, to provide the service effectively.

Equipment provision for schools has historically operated as a standalone service; this is partly because of the different funding and commissioning arrangements. This should not now be so much of an issue with pooled budgets being developed as part of local joint health and wellbeing strategies, together with the fact that Health and Wellbeing Boards now have a duty to promote integrated working right across the spectrum, including housing and education.

Although this section has been developed particularly for special schools the principles also apply where equipment is provided to service users in mainstream schools.

36.1 There is evidence that equipment provided in schools is subject to all relevant health and safety and medical devices regulations.

36.2 Equipment is electronically recorded, traceable, and is subject to planned maintenance scheduling arrangements.

36.3 Formal commissioning/contracting arrangements exist for the provision of community equipment in schools.

36.4 There is an allocated budget for the provision of children's specialist disability equipment.

36.5 There are protocols in place for the funding of communication equipment.

36.6 There are robust monitoring arrangements in place to ensure equipment can be shared outside the school environment, e.g. at home.

36.7 All relevant standards relating to mainstream and routine equipment provision, as set out within this Code of Practice, are also adhered to when providing equipment in schools.

CODE STANDARD 37

Complex, Specialist and Children's Equipment

OUTCOME

Service users requiring complex, specialist or children's equipment are assessed appropriately, and provided with suitable equipment in a safe and timely manner.

Introduction to Code standard 37

The provision of complex, specialist and children's equipment is commonly recognised as a very large and complicated area which can cause many difficulties in service delivery.

Poor service provision directly impacts upon the lives and wellbeing of many vulnerable individuals right across the health, social care and education spectrum.

Often problems occur with providing this type of equipment because it is usually expensive. Limiting provision because of funding restraints can be a short-sighted view as not providing this type of equipment appropriately and in a timely manner can often be much more costly in leading to secondary and unnecessary, episodes of care. Some common issues arising from poor provision include:

- unacceptable quality leading to unnecessary episodes of care, e.g. hospitalisation, admission to care homes
- a loss of access to schools, and impaired length and quality of life (children)
- exposure to litigation and prosecution for non-compliance with civil and criminal legislation

- services being unnecessarily costly and unsustainable, by failing to exploit scale economies, collaboration or sharing of resource.

Equipment can range from children's postural support equipment to bariatric beds, communication aids and sensory impairment aids – basically all non-routine community equipment.

Regardless of the difficulties encountered with these types of equipment and associated services, organisations are still required to comply with the same legal and welfare obligations as those for routine equipment.

It should now be easier to address these difficult areas as Health and Wellbeing Boards have a duty to promote integrated working between health, social care, housing and education, agencies.

37.1 There are formal and suitable arrangements in place for dealing with all aspects of complex, specialist and children's equipment, including:

- commissioning and contracting
- funding
- operational issues, including purchasing, storage, decontamination, medical device management, planned maintenance scheduling, health and safety, delivery, and risk management
- training for staff in use of and repair of equipment.

37.2 All relevant standards relating to mainstream and routine equipment provision, as set out within this Code of Practice, are also adhered to for specialist & children's equipment.

CODE STANDARD 38

Continuing Healthcare Equipment
OUTCOME
Equipment provided for continuing healthcare needs is safe, suitable, and is covered by appropriate maintenance and breakdown arrangements.

Introduction to Code standard 38
Continuing healthcare is a general term that describes the care that children and adults need, over an extended period of time as a result of illness, accident or disability. It can address both physical and mental health needs.

Continuing healthcare can be provided in a range of settings, such as a hospital, a registered care home or a person's own home. The type of health care services provided include primary health care, respite health care, community health services, and health care equipment. The responsibility for provision of care and equipment lies with the NHS.

A person considered to be eligible for continuing healthcare will generally have: complex health care needs; and/or intensive health care needs; and/or unstable/unpredictable health care needs; rapid deterioration. Qualifying individuals will also require significant health care inputs, such as regular supervision by a member of the NHS care team (e.g. a therapist), and routine use of specialist health care equipment.

The difficulty with the equipment provided for continuing healthcare service users is that it is quite often very specialist, e.g. ventilator. The equipment therefore requires rigorous safety checks and support. However, because this type of equipment does not usually go through the usual community equipment service route, the maintenance and support, where provided, is usually provided directly by suppliers. This means that equipment responsibilities, e.g. planned maintenance schedules, can sometimes be overlooked, and in some cases completely ignored. This is a huge risk to the service user as some of this equipment is life supporting, and to the responsible organisation in terms of risk.

38.1 There are formal and suitable arrangements in place for dealing with all aspects of continuing healthcare equipment, including:

- commissioning and contracting
- funding (whole life costs, e.g. maintenance, calibration, specialist decontamination)
- operational issues, including purchasing, storage, decontamination, medical device management, planned maintenance scheduling, health and safety, delivery, and training for staff in use of and repair of equipment
- the ability to recall equipment if necessary.

38.2 Where equipment is ordered directly from the supplier, to go to a service user's home, there are suitable medical device management arrangements in place, including all aspects of maintenance and breakdown cover. This is supported by an in-house database showing where equipment is, and when it next requires maintenance.

38.3 Any equipment ordered has the approval of medical device management boards, or similar in-house technical authority.

38.4 Service users are provided with user instructions, together with information outlining what to do in the event of product failure, or failure of ancillary supplies needed for the equipment to function, for example.

38.5 All relevant standards relating to mainstream and routine equipment provision, as set out within this Code of Practice, are also adhered to for continuing healthcare equipment.

CODE STANDARD 39

Community Equipment in Care Homes

OUTCOME

There is clarity around the roles, responsibilities, obligations and legal requirements where community equipment is provided into a care home.

Introduction to Code standard 39

There is often a lack of clarity in terms of roles and responsibilities for providing community equipment into care homes. Consequently some local areas develop their own protocol for equipment provision into care homes. Whatever the approach, there are clear legal responsibilities which must be addressed, e.g. health and safety, medical device management.

Where a community equipment service provides equipment into a care home they are still expected to meet all relevant health and safety, and medical device management responsibilities, e.g. planned maintenance and repairs, unless formal arrangements have been put in place to transfer those responsibilities to the care home.

Even without a transfer of responsibilities, the care home should still be expected to clean the equipment regularly, whilst in use, and comply with relevant manufacturer's instructions for the equipment whilst in use.

39.1 Where equipment is provided by organisations into care homes there is a clear protocol setting out roles and responsibilities for both parties. Care homes are made aware of this protocol, before its introduction. The protocol includes, but is not limited to:

- cleaning responsibilities (whilst in use)
- planned maintenance responsibilities, e.g. LOLER testing
- emergency breakdown cover, including out of hours
- guidance on following manufacturer's instructions
- contact details.

39.2 There is a list available of equipment types and eligibility criteria for equipment provision into care homes, for relevant staff and organisations to refer to.

39.3 Terms and conditions are agreed before equipment is issued into the care home. Care homes are expected to sign this, either upon receipt of equipment or as part of an overall contract. This specifies the responsibilities of both parties, and the conditions which must be met before equipment can be issued. It includes for example:

Acknowledgement that:
- all pieces of equipment remain the property of the community equipment service at all times
- the pieces of equipment received are for the sole use of the patient named on the requisition for equipment
- the residential/care home will advise the community equipment service when the resident no longer has need of the equipment
- the residential/care home accepts responsibility for all risks should the equipment be used by any patient other than the person for whom the item was requested
- the care home will pay for any lost items, or any damaged or broken equipment through negligence or misuse.

39.4 All relevant standards relating to mainstream and routine equipment provision, as set out within this Code of Practice, are also adhered to for equipment provision within care homes.

CODE STANDARD 40

Hospital Discharge Arrangements
OUTCOME
Provision of necessary community equipment is a seamless part of hospital discharge.

Introduction to Code standard 40

There are many community equipment related reasons why delayed hospital discharges can occur, for example:

- delayed and problematic service user requirements and home assessments
- arranging suitable times and dates, etc. for equipment to be delivered and/or installed in the service user's home
- adaptations, complex, specialist and/or children's equipment are required
- complex packages of care involving different health and social care agencies
- equipment package provided from different sources, e.g. retailer and statutory community equipment store
- cross border difficulties, i.e. discharging a service user into a different county/Local Authority boundary
- poor communication and formal arrangements between hospital and community based staff
- funding issues.

Whatever the reason for delays it is clearly important to ensure robust and streamlined systems and procedures exist to minimise delays. It is also important to ensure that whatever procedures are used, these are widely communicated and understood.

40.1 Both hospital and community based staff work to mutually agreed hospital discharge assessment and access criteria to manage users both with temporary impairment and chronic, permanent conditions.

40.2 Hospital staff responsible for discharging service users are trained in both the assessment and the provision aspects of community equipment.

40.3 Where service users require community equipment to facilitate a hospital discharge the process is reflected within a mutually agreed policy between hospital and community based health and social care organisations. This includes a communication plan with community staff, and also community equipment services. This reflects the operational functions of the community equipment services, e.g. contact details, opening hours, delivery schedules. It also includes cross border arrangements, and links with different agencies.

40.4 Where the TCES Retail Model is in place there is a protocol demonstrating the ordering and delivery processes where a service user needs equipment from different sources to enable a hospital discharge. This links to the hospital discharge policy.

40.5 All relevant standards relating to mainstream and routine equipment provision, as set out within this Code of Practice, are also adhered to when discharging service users from hospital with community equipment.

CODE STANDARD 41

Direct Payments
OUTCOME

Anyone receiving a direct payment for community equipment will do so in a straightforward and timely manner; they will also be given clear guidance around ownership responsibilities, including breakdown, maintenance and disposal.

Introduction to Code standard 41

Where offered, direct payments are a different way of obtaining some community equipment and/or minor adaptations needed to help individuals to live more independently. Instead of statutory organisations providing equipment and/or minor adaptations, money is given to the individual in the form of a direct payment enabling individuals to purchase equipment themselves.

One of the advantages of a direct payment is that individuals may choose to buy the equipment from a different supplier to the one the statutory organisation uses, or to put the money towards a more costly, highly specified model.

Individuals do not have to receive a direct payment if they prefer the statutory organisation to provide the equipment and/or minor adaptation for them.

Direct payments must be spent on meeting the service user's assessed needs.

Generally speaking equipment acquired using a direct payment will belong to the service user, and they will be responsible for its care and maintenance – although discretionary rules can apply relating to ownership and maintenance to reflect the best interest of the service user. Also, in some instances additional sums of money will be added to the initial payment to cover a warranty, as well as ongoing maintenance, etc.

41.1 Agencies offering direct payments have a clear policy and procedure in place for staff and potential service users to be able to access.

41.2 Agencies offering direct payments have a user agreement in place which clearly sets out how the direct payment should be used. Information within an agreement includes, but is not excluded to: Names and addresses, conditions of the agreement, payment arrangements and user's contribution, proof of sale, warranty, review details, maintenance, ownership and disposal.

41.3 Where direct payments are provided, the need for training is covered in the direct payment agreement.

41.4 All relevant standards relating to mainstream and routine equipment provision, as set out within this Code of Practice, are also adhered to when providing equipment using a direct payment arrangement.

CODE STANDARD 42

Links to Related Services, e.g. Wheelchairs, Telecare

OUTCOME

Community equipment providers communicate effectively and collaborate with other equipment related services, to reduce delays and duplication for service users.

Introduction to Code standard 42

Quite often similar equipment related entities, e.g. wheelchair services, community equipment services, and housing departments, provide separate services to the same service user. This can result in separate assessments and equipment provision, involving duplication in time, cost and effort. Similarly there are cases where different clinical professionals, e.g. occupational therapists, district nurses and physiotherapists, make separate assessments for the same service user. Having several assessments and several deliveries of equipment can be disconcerting for the service user, and are a poor use of resource in terms of the clinical professionals' time.

In addition, equipment related data and information for the different equipment services are generally held separately. As a result of this, one database may show a service user as having some community equipment, another may show the service user having a wheelchair, and another may show the service user having other items of assistive technology, e.g. Telecare. It is difficult to look at the total equipment care package collectively.

These difficulties may also be compounded in regions that have implemented the TCES Retail Model, where for example a service user may require some equipment from their in-house store and the remainder from a retailer. Unless there are systems in place for recording what has been issued to the service user, clinical professionals will not have a complete picture of the equipment service users have access to.

It is understood that it is not possible to have one assessment which covers all aspects of a service user's equipment needs, nor is it always practical to have all the information relating to a service user's equipment on a single database.

However there are potential synergies and reduced duplication of effort to be had by streamlining the processes.

There will be scope under the health and wellbeing strategies to link various equipment related services. This will include health, social care, education and housing.

42.1 The health and wellbeing strategy and/or the service specification for the provision of community equipment services include links to associated services, e.g. wheelchair services, outlining how services will work in collaboration to ensure duplication is minimised, and that services are provided as efficiently and timely as possible.

42.2 Suitable arrangements are in place to ensure assessments and equipment deliveries are minimised to reduce the number of contacts experienced by the service user.

42.3 Where services are working jointly there is a database, or cross reference data available, in an accessible format, to ensure clinical professionals can view all the equipment possessed by service users.

42.4 Where the TCES Retail Model is adopted, information is available to show what equipment the service user has.

42.5 There is a clear communication plan in place to ensure equipment care packages coming from different sources, e.g. equipment stores and retailers are co-ordinated.

CODE STANDARD 43

Third Party Contractors
OUTCOME
All third party contractors have their contractual, quality and performance related requirements clearly communicated and documented, and these are closely monitored and reviewed on a regular basis.

Introduction to Code standard 43
It is common for some aspects of community equipment services to be provided by third party contractors. This may be the provision of logistics or decontamination processes for example; in some cases a significant part of the equipment service may be provided by a third party. In these cases it is still important to ensure that all legal obligations are being met, as outsourcing parts of service provision does not in any way reduce statutory duties and responsibilities. It is important therefore that, no matter what aspects are undertaken by third party providers, responsibilities are clearly set out from the beginning, and there are measures in place for ensuring that those responsibilities are being met. Third party contractors will also include retailers where they are carrying out statutory functions on behalf of the public sector.

43.1 Where components of community equipment services are outsourced to third party contractors this is formally and mutually agreed, as appropriate, e.g. contract, service level agreement, memorandum of understanding.

43.2 Third party service providers have been made aware of the legal responsibilities they are expected to meet. This is in place prior to contract award, or commissioning of service provision, and is mutually agreed.

43.3 Where third party services are operating they are subject to the same contract management processes as in-house providers, e.g. quality and performance management reports, together with relevant key performance indicator compliance, as appropriate.

43.4 Staff employed by third party providers are subject to the same requirements as in-house services, e.g. Criminal Record Bureau (CRB) checks, staff training.

CODE STANDARD 44

Outsourced Service Providers

OUTCOME

Where services are fully outsourced all contractual, responsibility, liability, accountability, quality and performance related issues are mutually agreed and clearly documented.

Introduction to Code standard 44

Some community equipment services are outsourced to external providers, as an alternative way of providing services. This approach is sometimes viewed as passing the responsibility from the statutory provider to the external provider. This is only partly true as the ultimate responsibility for ensuring service users get a satisfactory service, and that their needs are being met, still lies with the statutory provider.

Where the TCES Retail Model has been adopted, especially where complex equipment provision has also been outsourced to different suppliers/providers, it is important for clear responsibilities to be defined. This may be in the form of a written contract, or where the retailer is concerned, at least set out within a 'Memorandum of Understanding.'

As well as the traditional health and social care in-house community equipment providers there are also different types of hosting providers emerging, e.g. independent and private sector, social enterprises - including Local Authority trading companies.

Regardless of how services are provided, it ultimately remains the responsibility of the commissioners to ensure that what they are expecting the external provider to do has been clearly stipulated, mutually agreed upon and formally contracted, including a service specification, for example.

There can sometimes be the assumption that outsourced external providers will know what they have to provide without actually being asked to do it. Fundamentally the external provider cannot be expected to provide services they have not been properly commissioned, contracted or paid to deliver. It is therefore essential that all expectations and service requirements are clearly specified before any form of contract takes place.

44.1 Outsourced services are subject to the same commissioning and services provision standards as in-house providers, as set out in this Code of Practice.

CODE STANDARD 45

Involvement of Users and Carers

OUTCOME

The commissioning, design, performance standards and product selection of community equipment involves service users and/or carers as a matter of course.

Introduction to Code standard 45

The provision of community equipment services is ultimately to assist and support clinical services in the delivery of appropriate care to service users. It is therefore important that the views of users, and their carers, are taken into account when planning, designing or reviewing service provision. Views may be captured by directly involving users and carers on various groups, e.g. HealthWatch, or by gaining feedback through questionnaires.

The involvement of service users and carers in the development of community equipment services is crucial. They can make a contribution at several levels. As individuals they can contribute from their own experience of using the services. This information may be gathered during the assessment process, at the review stage or via some form of survey.

Service users and carers can also contribute by being involved in the planning and development of the service through representation on the various forums charged with developing services, e.g. Health and Wellbeing Boards. Ideally the views of service users and carers should be included in the joint strategic needs assessment, and subsequently factored into any joint health and wellbeing strategies.

45.1 There is evidence that commissioners/planning teams, providers and clinical teams have taken input from service users and/or carers when developing services, strategies and policies. Some example roles and responsibilities of service users include:

- input into the development of the joint strategic needs assessment and joint health and wellbeing strategy
- interpret policy into service delivery
- reviews of assessment facilities and new equipment
- review outcomes from questionnaires and surveys, etc.
- analyse and review compliments and complaints
- advise on local and national disability policies and/or legislation.

45.2 Where appropriate, service users and/or carers are actively informed and involved in the development of equipment specifications, the equipment review and selection processes, and in a formal feedback process about the overall satisfaction with service provision.

CODE STANDARD 46

Cross Border Protocol

OUTCOME

Suitable arrangements exist to ensure service users who require community equipment and who are affected by geographical boundaries have their equipment needs met in a safe, co-ordinated and timely manner.

Introduction to Code standard 46

Cross border issues can be very problematic when providing community equipment, especially where there are no clear guidelines about geographical areas of responsibility. Problems generally stem from the difference between Local Authorities providing services to all residents within county boundaries, whereas the NHS often works to postcodes or GP surgeries' registered service users. Problems arising from this issue are far reaching and impact upon many areas of care where equipment is required. Some examples of these include:

- hospital discharges
- disabled children and young people in special schools, children's homes or in foster care
- residential and nursing homes
- respite care
- service users moving home.

In view of the new commissioning arrangements within the NHS, together with the Health and Wellbeing Boards, where health, Local Authorities and other strategic partners will be represented, there is an opportunity to address some of the longstanding cross-border issues.

46.1 There is a local cross border protocol in existence outlining the following areas of responsibility:

- the geographical area where community equipment will be provided
- funding and recharging for out of county arrangements
- service responsibilities for county residents outside the county, e.g. at university, special schools
- residential and nursing home provision
- communication protocol
- process for making referrals
- relevant contact details for community equipment providers, including opening hours, for example
- the types of equipment that will be provided by the various services, e.g. beds and hoists.

CODE STANDARD 47

Disabled Facilities Grants (DFGs) and Major Adaptations
OUTCOME
Service users requiring major adaptations and a Disabled Facilities Grant are assessed appropriately, and provided with suitable equipment in a safe, co-ordinated and timely manner.

Introduction to Code standard 47
A Disabled Facilities Grant (DFG) is a means tested grant designed to help meet the costs of adaptations to a property for a disabled occupant. In order to qualify for a DFG the required adaptations need to be considered *necessary and appropriate* (by the housing department, but on a recommendation by social services) to meet the needs of the disabled person; and it must be considered *reasonable and practicable* (by the housing department) for the relevant works to be carried out.

The provisions covering mandatory Disabled Facilities Grant (DFGs) are detailed in the Housing Grants, Construction and Regeneration Act 1996, as amended by the Regulatory Reform (Housing Assistance) Order 2002.

The Housing Grants, Construction and Regeneration Act 1996 states that Disabled Facilities Grants must be given to provide facilities deemed necessary and appropriate to meet the needs of the disabled person.

Some of the types of work carried out under a DFG include: have easier access to and from the property; have easier access to a room used or that can be used as a bedroom; have easier access to a room in which there is a toilet, bath or shower. Major Adaptations are usually in excess of £1,000, and can be anywhere up to £30,000 in value, and include for example: ramps, stairlifts, vertical lifts, door widening, level access shower, overhead ceiling track hoists. The maximum mandatory award for a DFG is £30,000. As this grant is means tested, some people may have to pay a contribution towards the required work themselves. However, under the Regulatory Reform (Housing Assistance) Order 2002, local housing authorities have discretion, but not a duty, to exceed the £30,000 amount.

Generally speaking these types of services are carried out by home improvement agencies, e.g. Care and Repair, or external contractors, on behalf of Local Authorities. Although there is a similarity in nature, and sometimes an overlap, between these services and providers of community equipment, they are generally provided outside the normal route for the provision of community equipment.

There is often ambiguity surrounding certain aspects of major adaptation provision as, for example, who has responsibility for funding certain aspects of works, supplier contracts and on-going maintenance.

One of the main criticisms of DFGs is the length of time it takes from referral through to approval. In some cases this can be up to two years. Some of the reasons for these delays include: service users' availability, property ownership, financial resources, landlords' consent, building regulations approval, and obtaining detailed quotations for the agreed works.

Under the Housing Grants, Construction and Regeneration Act 1996, Local Authorities should provide an answer to an application for a DFG as soon as is reasonably practicable, and no later than six months after the application is made. The actual payment of the DFG should take place no more than 12 months after the application was made.

Local Authorities have a duty to try to reduce any problems or suffering caused by the lack of suitable accommodation while a DFG is being considered. This can include providing funding for a temporary move to more suitable accommodation.

47.1 An efficient, consistent and timely adaptations service is provided.

47.2 A range of major adaptations are on offer to assist service users to remain safe and comfortable, and to maintain their independence within their own homes.

47.3 Assistance is given to those in need of adaptations to make informed choices about their housing options, facilitating transfers to more appropriate accommodation where required.

47.4 The adaptations required are considered along with the service user's priority. Prioritisation is based on the needs of the individual and any existing health and safety risks to the individual and/or their carer.

47.5 Assistance is offered to households whose current home is unsuitable for major adaptations. Where only extensive, costly adaptations will meet the particular needs of a household, rehousing options are considered.

47.6 All adaptation work completed on a property is recorded to ensure future allocations of the property are made to applicants requiring such adaptations wherever practicable.

47.7 Contractors carrying out adaptations will be closely monitored by those with the right technical skills to ensure the work meets the required standard, complies with the Occupational Therapist's original recommendation and takes the service user's needs into account.

47.8 There is clarity around the responsibility for the servicing and on-going maintenance of all adaptations.

47.9 Service users are kept informed about the progress of their DFG and adaptation, and their views are sought on their satisfaction with completed works.

47.10 The DFG policy is reviewed on a regular basis in line with legislative or regulatory changes.

47.11 Where an adaptation is required a process seeking formal agreement is followed. This may include the service user, carer, other members of the household, and other appropriate agencies.

Appendices

Appendix 1   101
The legal and welfare framework relating to community equipment

Appendix 2   125
Guide for contract management indicators

Appendix 3   129
SEMTA Occupational Standards specifically for community equipment
technicians

Appendix 4   131
Supporting guidance relating to training on Information Systems and
Information Management for individual roles

Appendix 5   133
Supporting guidance relating to Medical Device Management

Appendix 6   143
Health and Safety Executive (HSE) 'POPMAR' Model

Appendix 7   145
Supporting guidance relating to the choice of decontamination method
appropriate to the degree of infection risk associated with the intended
use of the equipment

Appendix 8   147
Glossary

Appendix 1
The legal and welfare framework relating to community equipment

LEGAL/WELFARE REQUIREMENTS	RELEVANCE TO COMMUNITY EQUIPMENT SERVICES	POSSIBLE LEGAL BREACHES
Overarching health and safety, governance and legal obligations		
UN Convention on the Rights of Disabled People (Signed and ratified by the UK). This Convention is known as The Rights of Persons with Disabilities in other parts of the United Nations. The Office for Disability Issues chose to retitle this for its use in the UK.	The main purpose of the Convention is to promote, protect and ensure the full and equal enjoyment of all human rights and fundamental freedoms by all persons with disabilities, and to promote respect for their inherent dignity. It is a requirement for partnership boards/commissioners and community equipment providers to ensure their service provision reflects and indeed includes: Participation and Inclusion, Non-discrimination, Accessibility, Personal mobility and rehabilitation issues, as set out in the Convention	Failing to provide a service to certain service user groups would most certainly breach the Convention rules, e.g. children requiring equipment to access the education system. Failing to provide equipment to certain service user groups whose needs have been assessed, but are not provided with equipment, particularly when the need fits within the eligibility criteria, could also be in breach of the Convention.
The UN Convention on the Rights of the Child (UNCRC)	The UN Convention is an international human rights treaty that applies to all children and young people aged 18 and under. It is the most widely ratified international human rights instrument and gives children and young people a wide range of civil, political, economic, social and cultural rights which State Parties	Failing to provide necessary equipment and support to children and their carers might be considered to be in breach of the Convention. Failure also to ensure

eligibility criteria is in keeping with the requirements of the Convention, and Article 23 in particular, may also be considered as a breach of the Convention.

to the Convention are expected to implement.

Article 23 contains sections with particular relevance to community equipment provision, as follows:

1. State Parties recognize that a mentally or physically disabled child should enjoy a full and decent life, in conditions which ensure dignity, promote self-reliance and facilitate the child's active participation in the community.

2. State Parties recognize the right of the disabled child to special care and shall encourage and ensure the extension, subject to available resources, to the eligible child and those responsible for his or her care, of assistance for which application is made and which is appropriate to the child's condition and to the circumstances of the parents or others caring for the child.

3. Recognizing the special needs of a disabled child, assistance extended in accordance with paragraph 2 of the present article shall be provided free of charge, whenever possible, taking into account the financial resources of the parents or others caring for the child, and shall be designed to ensure that the disabled child has effective access to and receives education, training, health care services, rehabilitation services, preparation for employment and recreation opportunities in a manner conducive to the child's achieving the fullest possible social integration and individual development, including his or her

cultural and spiritual development.

4. State Parties shall promote, in the spirit of international co-operation, the exchange of appropriate information in the field of preventive health care and of medical, psychological and functional treatment of disabled children, including dissemination of and access to information concerning methods of rehabilitation, education and vocational services, with the aim of enabling State Parties to improve their capabilities and skills and to widen their experience in these areas. In this regard, particular account shall be taken of the needs of developing countries.

| Corporate Manslaughter Act 2007 | In summary, an organisation is guilty of Corporate Manslaughter if the way in which its activities are managed or organised causes a death and amounts to a gross breach of a relevant duty of care to the deceased. A substantial part of the breach must have been in the way activities were managed by senior management – which would most likely be partnership board members/commissioners.

The offence is particularly concerned with organisations, including partnerships. Individuals can still be prosecuted separately for health and safety negligence by, for example, the Health and Safety Executive – and by the Crown Prosecution Service for gross negligence manslaughter in common law.

The law therefore allows for collective decisions like, for | The Health and Safety Executive (HSE) writes concerning the Corporate Manslaughter Act that:

'Companies and organisations should keep their health and safety management systems under review, in particular, the way in which their activities are managed and organised by senior management.'

In view of this, a potential breach could be the partnership board/commissioners failing to |

	example, partnership board decisions. For the offence to apply, an organisation must have owed a "relevant duty of care" to the victim. The Act defines a duty of care as "…an obligation that an organisation has to take reasonable steps to protect a person's safety". This includes for example equipment used by employees, systems of work, products and services supplied to customers – or in this case, service users. Some of the 'duties' outlined within section 2 of the Act are connected to: supplying goods and services; commercial activities; construction and maintenance work; using or keeping plant, and vehicles. All of these could be relevant to the day-to-day activities carried out by community equipment services.	specify or have any controls in place for managing high risk areas, e.g. not getting equipment maintained to save on cost. This is quite a broad area but the most obvious factors which could potentially lead to a breach are serious failings with: Health and Safety at Work Act etc. 1974, Management of Health and Safety at Work Regulations 1999, and the governance arrangements in place.
Human Rights Act 1998 (European Convention on Human Rights)	This relates more to the decision making process of the community equipment service, from both the commissioner, prescriber and provider of the service. These must ensure that people have the right not to be subjected to 'inhuman or degrading treatment' – see article 3 for further details. In addition article 8 outlines the right to respect for home, family and private life. Article 14 suggests that there should be freedom from any form of discrimination.	'Discretionary decisions, including omissions to act, (i.e. all policy making, practices, procedures, actions, individual decisions) will become potentially challengeable for a breach of human rights'.[26] Where the consequences of not providing a piece of equipment

---

[26] www.careandhealthlaw.com (Accessed January 2009).

	have been made clear, where the service user would be subjected to inhuman/degrading circumstances, e.g. having to urinate in the living room - assuming the service user has been assessed and is eligible – and a decision is made not to supply, there could in some circumstances be a potential breach of the Act/Convention.	Examples of breaches might be excluding certain service user groups because of complicated or costly equipment needs, e.g. not providing equipment to children with complex disabilities without clinical justification, or people in end of life circumstances. Making access and information relating to services very difficult for certain client groups would be in breach of the Equality Act.
Equality Act 2010	From 1 October 2010, the Equality Act replaced the Disability Discrimination Act (DDA) 1995. One of the aims of the Equality Act 2010 is to protect disabled people and prevent disability discrimination. It provides legal rights for disabled people in the areas of: • employment • education • access to goods, services and facilities including larger private clubs and land based transport services • buying and renting land or property • functions of public bodies, for example the issuing of licences.	

Similar to DDA 1995 requirements the Equality Act 2010 states that providers of goods and services to the public, including NHS and Local Authorities, have a duty not to discriminate or provide less favourable treatment on grounds relating to a person's disability. This therefore applies to commissioners and clinical staff responsible for deciding what service user groups and equipment types will and will not be provided.

The Equality Act also provides rights for people not to be directly discriminated against or harassed because they have an association with a disabled person. This can apply to a carer or parent of a disabled person. In addition, people must not be directly discriminated against or harassed because they are wrongly perceived to be disabled.

Furthermore, disabled people's accessibility rights are enshrined in the Equality Act 2010:

- rights not to be discriminated against or harassed in *access to health services and social services*

- Adjustments have to be made for *accessing services* where it is reasonable for the service provider to do so, including information being in an *accessible* format

- Goods, services, facilities and premises are *accessible*

In addition, under s.149 of the Act, Local Authorities and NHS bodies must carry out what are broadly referred to as disability

Health and Safety at Work Act etc. 1974	impact assessments in relation to their policies and their effects on disabled people.
	Health and Safety at Work Act etc 1974, s.2. Employers have a duty to ensure, so far as is reasonably practicable, the health, safety and welfare at work of all their employees.

Duty of employers to non-employees: Health and Safety at Work Act etc 1974, s.3. Every employer has a duty to conduct its undertaking in such a way as to ensure, so far as is reasonably practicable, that people not in its employment but who may be affected by the undertaking are not thereby exposed to risk to their health and safety.

Section 2 of the Health and Safety at Work Act etc 1974 looks at the 'General duties of employers to their employees', and includes activities carried out in the community. Section 3 covers users and carers by outlining the 'General duties of employers and self-employed to persons other than their employees'. Basically Section 3 states the duty of employers to ensure persons *not* in their employment are not exposed to risks (so far as is reasonably practicable) to their health and safety, and also it is the responsibility of every employer to provide appropriate information to such individuals about the way undertakings are conducted which might affect their health and safety.

Particular relevance to community equipment provision under s.2 and s.3 would include such things as: appropriate acquisition |

	methods, inspecting, checking, recording, tracking, recall, training, maintenance, cleaning, storing, demonstrating, lifting operations, delivering, instructions, repair, replacement, and emergency call-out.	Failure to conduct any of the tasks listed opposite safely could potentially breach this Act. It is worth noting that there have already been some prosecutions relating to these types of issues, e.g. hoists, bedrails.
Management of Health and Safety at Work Regulations 1999	The regulations state: 'Every employer shall make a suitable and sufficient assessment of: (a) the risks to the health and safety of his employees to which they are exposed whilst they are at work; and (b) the risks to the health and safety of persons not in his employment arising out of or in connection by him of his undertaking'. The regulations also require all employers, and in this context community equipment partners/commissioners, to plan, organise, monitor and review work procedures. This also requires formal assessment of risks, especially where employees and any others might be affected by health and safety failures.	There would be a clear breach of these regulations if there was a serious untoward incident, and it was discovered that there were no written governance arrangements in place, including risk management processes. It is likely that poorly drafted contractual arrangements would also breach the regulations, in the event of an incident.
The Health and Safety (Offences) Act 2008	The Health and Safety Offences Act 2008 came into effect on 16 January 2009[27] and increased the number of circumstances in which employees may be imprisoned for health and safety	Failure to meet existing health and safety law could potentially breach this Act, although the

[27] This can be viewed at: www.opsi.gov.uk/acts/acts2008/plain/ukpga_20080020_en_2

	breaches. According to NHS Employers[28] the Act introduced tough new penalties to act as a deterrent to organisations that are tempted to flout the law. Certain offences are now triable in either the Magistrates' Court or the Crown Court. Employees could find themselves at risk of imprisonment under the law if they fail to take reasonable care of the health and safety of others or even themselves. In addition, a director and senior manager can infringe the law where the problem was caused with their consent, connivance or neglect. The highest fine that can be imposed by the lower courts has risen from £5,000 to £20,000. Higher courts can impose unlimited fines.	severity of the breach would be considered, e.g. serious neglect; reckless disregard for health and safety requirements; repeated breaches which create significant risks; false information and serious risks which have been deliberately created to increase profit.
Common law of negligence	The common law of negligence asserts that everyone owes a duty of care which requires one to consider the consequences of their acts and omissions and to ensure that those acts and/or omissions do not give rise to a foreseeable risk of injury to any other person. In simple terms it requires everyone to owe a duty not to injure other people by our negligent acts and omissions, and this is an individual duty which each of us owes all of the time to our 'neighbours', or those we are providing a service to. Obviously the relevance of this to community equipment provision is quite broad, but does however fit into almost every	An example of this might be that a serious untoward incident occurs where a service provider failed to maintain equipment in accordance with manufacturer's instructions.

---

[28] This can be viewed at: www.nhsemployers.org/practice/practice-4553.cfm

part of service delivery and commissioning.

A duty of care can be owed by both individual practitioners and also by organisations as a whole. In addition to their own duty of care, organisations will also be vicariously liable for the negligent acts of employees.

A failure to provide any equipment following an assessed need, which falls into the definition of the section (e) opposite, assuming the service users' needs fall within the eligibility criteria applied by the Local Authority, is likely to be in breach of the Act.

Welfare related obligations relevant to community equipment

| Chronically Sick and Disabled Persons Act 1970 | This relates specifically to the local social services authority in its legal obligations and provision of services in terms of assessment, for example. However community equipment will in a majority of cases be expected to meet the assessed equipment needs of the service user, e.g. ramps, adaptations.

The particular section within the Act which is most relevant to community equipment is section 2, paragraph (e):

(e) the provision of assistance for that person in arranging for the carrying out of any works of adaptation in his home or the provision of any additional facilities designed to secure his greater safety, comfort or convenience.

However, the other paragraphs of section 2, relating to other services, may also cover equipment. For example, making arrangements to: assist people to take advantage of educational facilities, for social and recreational facilities, for outings, for holidays, for travel, etc. |

NHS Act 1977 (supplanted by the NHS Act 2006 in England)	This relates specifically to the NHS as a whole in its legal obligations and provision of services. Community equipment provision will however in a majority of cases be expected to fulfil requests from NHS bodies in support of their obligations, e.g. community beds and mattresses for hospital discharges.	A potential breach may be difficult to specify in relation to community equipment provision for this Act. However, a failure to provide assessed equipment which supported the prevention of illness, or for the after care of the service user, e.g. beds for discharge, could possibly result in a breach of the Act. More specifically, however, the application of overly rigid, blanket policies about what services or equipment will or won't be provided could be unlawful on the grounds that the NHS body has "fettered its discretion".
NHS and Community Care Act 1990	Again this relates more to the assessment responsibilities and obligations of local social services authorities, although the assessed equipment needs will generally need to be supported by the provision of community equipment. See section 47 of the Act for details.	Failure to provide assessment, or adequate assessment, of a person's needs for equipment, could result in a breach of this Act.
Health and Social Care Act 2008	Section 57 of this Act makes it a duty for local social services authorities to make direct payments to people for non-residential	Failure to offer direct payments for equipment could be unlawful,

	services, including equipment and home adaptations - if certain conditions are met.	if the eligibility conditions for receiving a direct payment are otherwise met by the person.
Health Services and Public Health Act 1968	Under approvals made by the Secretary of State under section 45 of this Act, local social services authorities have a power to provide a range of non-residential services for older people generally. (As opposed to older, disabled people who would in any case fall under the Chronically Sick and Disabled Persons Act 1970). In particular authorities have a power, but no duty, to make arrangements to provide practical assistance in the home including assistance in the carrying out of works of adaptation or the provision of any additional facilities designed to secure greater safety, comfort or convenience.	To date, only powers rather than duties have been created under this Act. Failure to exercise such powers is unlikely to be unlawful.
National Assistance Act 1948	Section 21 of the National Assistance Act 1948 places a duty on Local Authorities to make arrangements for those in need of care and accommodation who are unable to make such arrangements themselves.	Failure to provide equipment which supports such arrangements could quite easily be a breach of the National Assistance Act.
Education Act 1996	Section 324 of the Act states that, within a statement of special educational needs, educational needs must be met – by the local education authority if nobody else (such as the NHS). In the case of non-educational needs, the authority has a power only. Educational needs are generally taken to apply to provision required to allow the child to follow the curriculum. This duty and this power could apply to equipment provision.	Under s.324, a failure by a local education authority to ensure provision (by itself or another body) of equipment - required to meet a specified educational need – could be unlawful.

	There are other more general duties relating to disabled children in the Education Act 1996 that could apply to the provision of equipment but which do not have the force of the s.324 duty.	A failure to provide services or equipment required by a child under s.17 of the 1989 Act is less likely to be held unlawful by the courts. They have consistently held the s.17 duty to be barely enforceable. However, in the case of a disabled child, the obvious enforceable duty would lie under s.2 of the Chronically Sick and Disabled Persons Act 1970, which applies to both adults and children. Failure to meet the equipment needs of a disabled child under s.22 or s.23 and the Fostering Services Regulations, could result in a finding of unlawfulness, as these duties focus on individual
Children Act 1989	Section 17 of the Children Act 1989 places a general duty on local social services authorities to safeguard and promote the welfare of children in need within their area. This widely drawn duty can include provision of equipment. It can also include provision not just for the child, but for any member of the family. Section 22 contains a more specific duty to safeguard and promote the welfare of any child legally looked after by the Local Authority. Section 23 contains a duty to provide accommodation for a child in Local Authority's care (including a child placed with family) and to maintain the child. If the child is disabled, there is a duty to ensure that the accommodation is not unsuitable for a child's particular needs. This could arguably include ensuring that the child has suitable equipment. The Fostering Services Regulations (SI 2002/57), made under s.22 of the Children Act, place a duty on fostering service providers to ensure that a child is provided with individual support, aids and equipment which the child may need because of health	

	needs or disability (r.15). There is also a duty on the provider to provide foster parents with training, advice, information, support (r.17).	children, rather than (as under s.17) the generality of children in need in the local area.
Fair Access to Care Services[29]	This relates particularly to eligibility criteria for adult social care, but should be considered when looking at joint eligibility criteria. Community equipment provision is bound to be supplied in support of the agreed eligibility criteria, e.g. critical, substantial. There is a responsibility upon those organisations providing community equipment to be able to provide the agreed criteria. There is also a responsibility for the commissioners (partnership boards) of these services to ensure the right eligibility criteria are both specified and met.	Fair access to care guidance is regarded as 'statutory' guidance. This means that although it is not law, nonetheless a failure to follow it could result in a finding of unlawfulness. For example, the English guidance states clearly that Local Authorities should not have blanket policies not to provide specific services (or, by implication, equipment). Many Local Authorities do have such blanket policies and are potentially in breach of the guidance. In addition, such blanket approaches may also be unlawful because they "fetter the discretion" of the authority – or because the effect of such policies

---

[29] Department of Health (2010), *Prioritising need in the context of Putting People First: a whole system approach to eligibility for social care - guidance on eligibility criteria for adult social care, England 2010.*

	may in some cases mean that a person's assessed, eligible, need is not met, contrary to the NHS and Community Care Act 1990 and the Chronically Sick and Disabled Persons Act 1970.	A failure to assess a carer's needs could clearly be unlawful.
Carers and Disabled Children Act 2000; Carers (Recognition and Services Act) 2005; and Carers (Equal Opportunities) Act 2004	The net effect of this legislation is that a local social services authority has a duty to assess the ability of an informal carer to care for an adult or child who may be in need of community care services, or services under Part 3 of the Children Act respectively. The duty is triggered if the carer is providing regular and substantial care and if he or she requests an assessment. The Local Authority must however tell carers about this right to assessment. The Local Authority must also consider the carer's involvement, or wish to be involved, in work, education, training, leisure. The Local Authority has a power to provide services, including equipment, for the carer. Other bodies, such as the NHS, have a duty to give due consideration to a request by the Local Authority in terms of assisting carers. The needs of a carer may be related to equipment, not only equipment being used by the person being cared for, but also by the carer in his or her own right. For instance, a mobile phone, a washing machine, manual handling training, or driving lessons.	

Community equipment providers - specific legal obligations		
Consumer Protection Act 1987 (Part 1)	Part 1 of the Consumer Protection Act 1987 transposes the Product Liability Directive (85/374/EEC and 1999/34/EC) into UK law. The legislation imposes strict liability on producers for harm caused by defective products. The legislation applies to all consumer products and products used at a place of work. The direct application to community equipment providers might be where it manufactures products, e.g. banisters.	There would be a case for breaching the Act where a product manufactured by a community equipment provider had a defect with the potential to cause harm. There may also be a case against community equipment providers if they modified equipment, which subsequently was issued with a defect in it, without first consulting the original manufacturer or following their guidance.
General Product Safety Regulations 2005	According to the Department for Business Enterprise and Regulatory Reform[30] (BERR), in principle, the 2005 Regulations apply to all products (new and second-hand) used by consumers, whether intended for them or not. The 2005 Regulations maintain the general duty placed on producers and distributors to place on the market (or supply) only products that are safe in normal or reasonable foreseeable use. The principal responsibility for day-to-day enforcement of	An obvious breach would be issuing unsafe products into the community, e.g. issuing equipment with exposure to electrical parts, walking frames that break easily, beds or chairs with exposure to entrapment.

[30] www.berr.gov.uk/whatwedo/consumers/Safety/products/general-regulations/index.html (Accessed January 2009)

		A serious breach of these regulations might be where an injury occurs to a driver, for example, who is expected to deliver a two person task single handed, e.g. beds. The case would be strengthened if there was no evidence of risk assessments or governance arrangements in place for monitoring and assessing risks. To avoid a breach there would need to be evidence to demonstrate: • attempts have been made to avoid the manual handling operation, so far as is reasonably practicable • where manual handling cannot be avoided, a suitable and sufficient risk assessment
	the Regulations lies with Local Authorities. For the first time, the Regulations recognise certain technical standards as carrying a presumption of conformity with the general safety requirement, meaning that products that comply with them are deemed to be safe.	
Manual Handling Operations Regulations 1992	This applies to any aspect of the service where a manual handling risk applies. In a community equipment provider setting this could be with a store, delivery, installation, maintenance or user or carer use of the equipment. For example a considerable amount of heavy equipment is required upstairs in people's homes, e.g. beds, hoists. The employer, or individual partners, will be responsible for ensuring all manual handling risks are avoided, where possible, which could otherwise result in injury. There should be appropriate risk assessments and governance arrangements in place, together with processes for monitoring and reviewing assessments on an on-going basis. Ideally these arrangements should be set out within the service specification. 'Where equipment is provided to reduce the risks involved in manual handling (e.g. hoists, slings, trolleys, etc.), it should go without saying that adequate training, information and	

	instructions on the use of the equipment must be provided. Merely providing such equipment (and any necessary training) will not absolve an employer from further responsibility or from liability: use of the equipment should be monitored and encouraged.'[31]	is carried out, factoring in the task, working environment, the physical capabilities of the individuals involved, and other relevant factors • appropriate steps have been taken to reduce the risk to health to the lowest level reasonably practicable.[32]
Medical Devices Regulations 2002 (Amended 2003)	These regulations require certain duties to be followed by manufacturers of equipment in particular, e.g. performance and safety standards, CE Marking. The direct application upon community equipment provision would be the standards to which they manufactured equipment, e.g. banisters, and also the difficulties arising from modifying CE marked equipment	Potential breaches could be: • manufacturing a substandard product • adapting or modifying certain pieces of equipment • acquiring equipment inappropriately, e.g. not CE marked.
Sale and Supply of Goods Act 1994	The Sale and Supply of Goods Act (which largely incorporates the Sale and Supply of Goods and Services Act 1982) requires a supplier of a service to carry out that service with reasonable care and skill and, unless agreed to the contrary, within a	Possible breaches may be easier to pinpoint if for example the equipment service was outsourced, although in-house services would also be expected to

---

[31] http://www.careandhealthlaw.com (Accessed January 2009).

[32] HSE. (2004). *Handling home care. Achieving safe, efficient and positive outcomes for care workers and service users.* Health and Safety Executive.

	reasonable time and make no more than a reasonable charge. The Act states that 'Any goods supplied in the course of the service must be as described, of satisfactory quality and fit for their purpose. If they are not, the consumer is entitled to a repair, replacement or compensation. A claim can be pursued through the courts for up to six years providing it can be shown that the problem was due to the work not being carried out properly or the goods or materials used not being of satisfactory quality. The most direct relevance to community equipment provision would be where a product is manufactured and issued to a service user from the service, e.g. banister. This might also be applicable where there are top-ups, direct payments or prescriptions issued by community equipment providers, or indeed where equipment is sold direct from a provider to the service user.	comply with quality, care, and skill elements. Where services use top-ups, or prescriptions, responsibility may lie with the commissioner to ensure service standards are specified.
MHRA Managing Medical Devices DB2006 (05) November 2006	In relation to the provision of equipment this is perhaps the most informative and comprehensive piece of guidance produced to date. It covers all aspects of managing medical devices. It also sets out recommended processes and directly relates to pertinent legislation, e.g. health and safety, consumer protection. In the unfortunate event of an untoward, fatal or serious accident, relating to any aspect of a medical device, it is very likely service standards would be investigated in line with the	This is a very comprehensive and explicit piece of guidance which has been made available for the specific purpose of managing medical devices. The guidance covers almost all aspects of medical device management relating to community equipment services, and assistive

	principles set out in this guidance. A serious breach of this guidance could potentially result in gross negligence or failed duty of care. This guidance should be in the possession of every partnership board/commissioner, and all providers of community equipment services.	technologies. The guidance points to all pertinent legislation and guidance in relation to community equipment services. It is likely that this guidance would be used as a benchmark in relation to performance if services were being inspected in the event of an untoward incident.
Lifting Operations and Lifting Equipment Regulations 1998 (LOLER)	Lifting equipment is defined as 'work equipment for lifting or lowering loads and includes attachments for anchoring, fixing or supporting it.' These regulations have a huge impact upon community equipment providers as a significant number of equipment categories fall under the LOLER remit, e.g. hoists, stairlifts. In many service areas there is great ambiguity around what should and what should not be subject to regular LOLER examination, e.g. beds, bathlifts. However one approach would be that whether equipment used at work is an item of lifting equipment should depend on a 'primary purpose' test; for instance, hoists and lifts are clearly lifting equipment, whereas an adjustable height bed is probably, primarily a bed and only	A clear breach of these regulations would be failing to carry out recommended LOLER inspections. It is also important to note that the regulations do not only cover the once or twice a year inspection, but also require such things as ensuring: • the equipment is of adequate strength and stability for the purpose it is to be used for • the equipment is positioned and installed appropriately • equipment is marked

	secondarily lifting equipment. Clearly there will be grey areas and, ultimately it would be for the courts to decide what is, and what is not, lifting equipment. However, all this need not cause equipment and adaptation providers undue concern, since the range of duties - including a strict duty of maintenance in the Provision and Use of Work Equipment Regulations 1998 apply in any case to all work equipment, not just lifting equipment.[33] Section 3 of the Health and Safety at Work etc Act 1974 more generally covers equipment subject to LOLER regulations in the service user's home. Section 3 would apply, however, in place of LOLER, if the lifting equipment were not being used "at work", because LOLER only applies in this latter circumstance. For example, if a hoist were being operated by an informal family carer, then it would not be equipment used at work and would fall under section 3 of the 1974 Act but not under LOLER. The Lifting Operations and Lifting Equipment Regulations 1998 impose further obligations relating to the examination and inspection, strength and stability, positioning and installation of equipment. There is also very much an overlap with PUWER regulations set out below.	appropriately with safe working loads, etc. • equipment defects are reported appropriately. In the event of an incident, failure to meet the above list could also warrant a breach of the regulations.
Provision and Use of Work Equipment Regulations 1998	PUWER requires all equipment used at work – including paid carers and clinical staff, etc. to be:	These Regulations make it the employer's responsibility to ensure work equipment is

---

[33] Mandelstam, M (2003). *Using the law to develop and improve equipment and adaptation provision*. The Stationery Office Bookshop, Edinburgh

(PUWER)	• suitable for the intended use and for conditions in which it is used • safe, maintained, inspected to ensure it continues to be safe • used only by the people who have received adequate information, instruction and training • accompanied with suitable safety measures, e.g. protective devices, markings, warnings. It is most likely that the commissioners would have to request compliance with these regulations, and that the provider would be responsible for meeting these. 'The Provision and Use of Work Equipment Regulations 1998 make it the employer's responsibility to ensure that work equipment is so constructed or adapted as to be suitable for the purpose for which it is used or provided. The regulations also impose a strict liability duty to maintain equipment in an efficient state, efficient working order and in good repair.'[34]	constructed or adapted in order to be suitable for the purpose for which it is used or provided. Possible breaches might be: • inappropriate assessments and equipment selection by clinical staff • equipment not maintained properly with planned preventative maintenance programmes in place • safety information and warnings not issued with equipment.
The Carriage of Dangerous Goods by Road Regulations 1996	This legislation requires strict control on many transporting arrangements. In relation to community equipment provision, consideration needs to be given to the packaging and handling of contaminated equipment, and segregation of clean and contaminated equipment. Securing of loads and safe methods of	Potential breaches could be some of the following; • inappropriate cleaning of vehicles • mixing clean and contaminated equipment

[34] www.careandhealthlaw.com (Accessed January 2009).

transportation would also have to be given consideration. This may also apply to clinical staff transporting equipment in their personal vehicles unsafely, or uninsured. It may even apply to service users or members of the public, being expected to unreasonably transport, or collect, their own equipment.	• unsuitable packaging • clinical staff using personal vehicles to transport equipment unsafely, or uninsured.
Control of Substances Hazardous to Health Regulations 2002 (COSHH)	In addition to the usual requirements within the workplace under this regulation, e.g. the management of chemicals or detergents, community equipment providers should strictly adhere to this regulation in relation to the control of biological agents such as bacteria and other dangerous micro-organisms. This regulation especially relates to infected or contaminated equipment. There should be clear policies and procedures developed to ensure potential infectious diseases are kept under control, e.g. protective clothing, decontamination/infection control guidance.	A most likely breach would be the failure to comply with COSHH requirements- especially in the event of an untoward incident. Failing in any of the following areas could result in a breach: • assessing risks • deciding on precautions needed • measures to prevent and control risks • ensuring control measures are used and maintained • monitoring exposure and health surveillance • informing, instructing and training employees about risks and precautions.

	It has been argued by some lawyers that COSHH regulations could apply to MRSA and Clostridium Difficile (CDiff) issues – although this may be difficult to prove at present. However failing to control substances likely to cause infection or contamination would be treading on dangerous ground.	An obvious breach of these regulations would be not to have any reporting mechanisms in place for allowing injuries to be reported There would also be serious breach of the regulations if injuries and dangerous occurrences, etc. were known about and purposely not reported.
The Reporting of Injuries, Diseases and Dangerous Occurrences Regulations 1995 (RIDDOR)	RIDDOR places a legal duty on employers and people in control of premises to: report work related deaths, major injuries or over three day injuries, work related diseases, and dangerous occurrences (near miss accidents). Equipment related injuries should be reported to the appropriate health and safety coordinator, or medical devices board. Community equipment partners/commissioners should ensure appropriate health and safety, risk management and governance arrangements are in place.	

Appendix 2

Guide for contract management indicators

(Note this section is for guidance only and does not form part of the Code of Practice).

Contract & Performance Management Indicator	What is being measured?
GENERAL	
Reasons for failing to deliver equipment within agreed timescale.	This information enables commissioners to manage service provision effectively by allowing them to focus on possible areas of weakness – which may be internal or external to the service provider. This information is crucial for effective contract management.
Waiting lists.	This shows the number of service users waiting for equipment. It also shows the length of time service users are waiting - particularly those who have fallen outside the performance indicator criteria. A reduction in the waiting lists shows progress in performance.
Stock value, turnaround, write-offs, collection rates and recycling levels.	These levels will have to be ascertained and agreed locally. Collection rates and recycling levels (where applicable) are most important as these indicate the efficiency of the provider.
MAINTENANCE	
Number of assets requiring maintenance (planned maintenance schedule) PAT & LOLER. Services should look to develop local targets for urgent repairs, e.g. 100% within 24hrs.	This helps to assess the performance of the provider; more importantly it highlights the level of risk to the service user and the organisation.

PROCUREMENT	
Performance measures should be developed around the following areas: • supplier performance (lead times etc.) • savings achieved • cost saving strategies through improved recall systems, recycling and improved maintenance scheduling.	This is in keeping with the overall partnership and integration agenda to provide an economical and efficient service. It informs commissioners how efficient the provider is.
QUALITY	
Quality improvement targets could be set for areas including: • number of complaints • service user satisfaction surveys • staff turnover • infection control (random spot checks) • quality control processes in place, e.g. policies and procedures.	These measures are most important as these determine the actual quality of the service being provided to the service user. Also good results for these help to sustain high levels of staff morale with subsequent low staff turnover, etc. All of these measures look at the quality outputs of the service from a governance, service user/staff satisfaction and overall provider performance perspective.
SAFETY	
Safety improvement targets could be set for areas including: • access to competent health and safety advice	All of these measures look at the safety outputs of the service for both service users and staff from a governance and health and safety perspective.

<ul><li>health and safety policies</li><li>risk assessments</li><li>evidence of staff training</li><li>incident and near miss investigation procedures.</li></ul>	

Appendix 3

SEMTA Occupational Standards specifically for community equipment technicians

(Note this section is for guidance only and does not form part of the Code of Practice).

SEMTA Occupational Standard Level 2 (or equivalent)

An individual who has completed Level 2 is assumed to be competent to perform the following tasks:

- Dismantle, remove and replace or repair faulty components, in line with company procedures, on a variety of different types of assistive technology systems and equipment, such as manual and powered wheelchairs, buggies and scooters, postural support systems, hoists, personal communication aids, walking aids, adjustable beds, pressure relief and distribution equipment, telecare alarm systems, aids for daily living, environmental control systems, associated battery charging systems for assistive technology systems and equipment;

- Cover a range of maintenance activities, such as isolating equipment, labelling components, dismantling components to the required level, setting and adjusting components, replacing or repairing components, carrying out functional checks and safety checks before handing over to the end user.

SEMTA Occupational Standard Level 3 (or equivalent)

An individual who has completed Level 3 is assumed to be competent to carry out the following tasks in addition to those for Level 2:

- Carry out servicing activities on mechanical and electromechanical assistive technology equipment, in accordance with approved procedures;

- Service a range of mechanical/electromechanical assistive technology equipment such as wheelchairs, hoists, stair lifts, seating, walking aids, adjustable beds, pressure redistribution cushions, ramps, and aids to daily living. This may involve dismantling, removing and replacing faulty equipment, at component or unit level, on a variety of different types of assistive technology equipment;

- Apply a range of dismantling and reassembly methods and techniques, such as mechanical fitting, fixing, fastening, soldering, crimping, harnessing, and securing cables and components;

- Comply with (internal) organisational policy and procedures for the servicing activities undertaken, and report any problems with the activities that cannot be personally resolved, or that are outside permitted authority, to the relevant people;

- Work with minimal supervision, taking personal responsibility for actions and for the quality and accuracy of the work carried out.

Appendix 4

Supporting guidance relating to training on Information Systems and Information Management for individual roles

(Note this section is for guidance only and does not form part of the Code of Practice)

This section sets out an example of the level of understanding and training requirements, particularly related to information systems, for the various roles involved in the provision of community equipment.

Management staff

Service Level Agreements and contract management reports, stock turnover, trend analysis, stock requisition, audit trails, cost allocation to budgets and virtual budget management, expenditure by referrer (e.g. scheme of delegation), key performance indicator reporting, including mitigation/exclusion reports, recalls including MHRA and HSE warnings and notices, planned maintenance management, satellite store management, waiting list management, mail-shots, batch reporting, user defined fields, e-procurement, export of data to other software packages, e.g. Excel.

Stores staff, administration, technicians and drivers

Delivery and return requests, recycling, asset management, asset type setup, service template setup, asset register, asset service and maintenance (planned maintenance schedule), managing stock levels (set stock alerts), multiple stores capability, process orders, assign stock, pick order, deliver order, and use of handheld devices, where appropriate.

Prescribers (clinical staff)

On-line ordering, on-line product catalogue viewing, stock information, user instructions, health and safety instructions, detailed product descriptions, and functions such as: request non-stock item, request a return, track a return, request a repair and track a repair.

Where community equipment services are working within a scheme of delegation using a pooled funding arrangement, or alternatively virtual budget management, senior clinical staff might need to be able to create, schedule, view, run and understand expenditure and activity reports.

Appendix 5

Supporting guidance relating to Medical Device Management[35]

(Note this section does not form part of the Code of Practice, but should be considered when developing policy or assessing compliance with medical device management issues)

Policies and procedures

In relation to community equipment provision the Medical Device Management group, or appropriate partnership or commissioning board, will have in place policies that address the following topics - note this list is not exhaustive:

- decontamination procedures
- procurement arrangements
- records, both manual and electronic
- adverse incident reporting, including responsible individuals
- actions required on MHRA's medical device alerts and manufacturers' corrective notices
- a named medical device lead with responsibility for responding to alerts
- training on use, assembly, installation, cleaning and disposal
- technical specifications
- regulatory compliance and related issues, e.g. Provision and Use of Work Equipment Regulations (PUWER).

Reporting incidents

MHRA rely on incidents relating to medical devices being reported by local agencies. When sufficient incidents have been reported MHRA may send out an alert to all agencies. It is most important therefore that individual organisations take this responsibility seriously, and that they have systems and processes in place which allow this to happen.

According to MHRA, information from adverse incident reporting suggests that factors having the greatest impact on the safety of devices involve the instructions issued by the manufacturer, their availability and clarity, the

---

[35] For full details relating to medical device management see: MHRA (2006). *Managing Medical Devices. Guidance for healthcare and social services organisations.* DB2006(05) only available on website: www.mhra.gov.uk.

design of equipment, the quality of training in the appropriate uses of devices and how well they are maintained and prepared.

The causes of incidents may include:

- inadequate instructions for use from the manufacturer
- poor training
- problems arising from the design or manufacturing process
- inappropriate local modifications or adjustments
- inadequate maintenance
- inadequate or inappropriate repairs or replacement parts
- unsuitable storage or use conditions
- inadequate end of life or scrapping information.

Any of the above list can result in very serious incidents. It is important that when incidents are reported the reason is provided.

Medical Devices Management Board

There should be a Medical Devices Management Board (MDMB) in place to develop and implement policies across the organisation. These will usually review the various medical device policies at least once a year. It is essential that a member of the MDMB represents the interests of community equipment services. It is also essential than any medical device related policy or procedure is endorsed by the MDMB. There should be adequate information networks in place to enable communication to and from the MDMB. Individuals involved should include: Service/store managers; technical staff; purchasing staff; clinical professionals.

Although much of this activity will be covered by internal audit teams, as part of the organisation's governance and risk management arrangements it is essential that community equipment provision is represented on the MDMB.

Acquisition processes

A fundamental part of medical device management is in the acquisition of community equipment. It is easy to assume that products are safe and of good quality just because they are sold or loaned from reputable suppliers.

Where one exists, the medical devices management group, or product selection group, should have local policies for the acquisition of medical devices to address safety, quality, and performance as well as all aspects of the acquisition cycle. Policies should include and take account of the needs and preferences of all interested parties, e.g. those involved in use, commissioning, purchasing, decontamination, maintenance and decommissioning. Policies will also factor in local and national acquisition policies, whole life costs, the method of acquisition (e.g. purchasing and/or leasing).

Where equipment is either on loan, trial or for assessment purposes it must be clear whose responsibility it will be should any problems arise.

In-house manufacture
Provider services that manufacture medical devices, e.g. banisters or ramps, but do not place them on the market should only do so in accordance with the Medical Devices Regulations - MHRA DB2006 (05).

Modifying and changing use
Modifying existing devices or using them for purposes not intended by the manufacturer (off-label use) has safety implications, especially in the event of an adverse incident. It may also count as manufacture of a new device under the Medical Devices Regulations, according to MHRA. Those undertaking modifications or changing the use of equipment should only do so in accordance with Medical Device Regulations - MHRA DB2006 (05). Modifications in use outside of the manufacturer's intended use will only be considered as part of a fully documented risk management process within the provider service risk management policy and procedures.

There are some organisations with the necessary specialist skills and experience for modifying and changing the use of equipment, so that the needs of service users with specific requirements can be met. For example 'Remap'[36] is a charity, working through a nationwide network of dedicated volunteers to provide this type of service. Remap's unique pieces of special equipment are tailor-made and given free to the people who need them. Remap already has 85 panels across England, Wales and Northern Ireland, and helps over 3000 people with disabilities each year.

[36] For further information visit: www.remap.org.uk

Where modifications are made to equipment or changing its use the following factors are considered:

Fitness for intended purpose/application
- whether the device is compatible with other devices, and any medicinal products that it is likely to be used with
- whether the manufacturer intends the device to be used by those who will be using it
- whether the device is appropriate for the intended environment.

Safety and performance
- has the equipment got a suitable CE-mark, ISO Standard
- is there evidence of past history problems with the equipment
- do MHRA safety publications, manufacturer's advisory notices or other relevant publications identify issues related to the device.

Maintenance support services
- can the equipment service provider (in-house or contractor) maintain the equipment
- is alternative equipment available to cover periods when equipment is being repaired or serviced
- are response times appropriate and guaranteed
- what are the proposed intervals between service, frequency and complexity of checks.

Training
The need for training depends upon the equipment and can involve users, carers or staff:
- will it be required for all anticipated users, carers or staff
- will it be required for maintenance and repair staff, to enable them to carry out these aspects.

Technical support
- does the manufacturer give free access to technical advice
- is there a 24-hour helpline
- is there a troubleshooting list supplied with equipment.

Support services
- is the installation to be carried out by manufacturer/supplier
- what building and utility services are required
- is special decontamination or calibration needed
- what other associated equipment is needed.

Second hand community equipment

Usage and service history should always be available for prospective purchasers before sale and then supplied with the equipment at the point of sale. As a minimum there should be a:

- record of any reconditioning work carried out, including a record of replacement parts
- copy of all maintenance and servicing that has been carried out including the name of maintenance/servicing organisation, including record of usage and decontamination status.

Electrical safety testing (portable appliance testing)

The provider's medical device management policy will cover the provision of maintenance and repair of all medical devices, including reconditioning and refurbishment. This will include for example:

- how each category of equipment should be maintained and repaired, and by whom
- the timescale for planned preventative maintenance, e.g. full service every 12 months and a visual inspection every 6 months
- the timescale for repairs to be completed, e.g. urgent repairs to be dealt with within 12 hours
- the frequency and type of planned preventive maintenance should be specified, taking account of the manufacturer's instructions, the expected usage and the environment in which it is to be used.

Training for professional and end users

Medical device policy will clearly set out the training requirements for professional users, e.g. therapist, and the user (e.g. service user or carer).

Professional users

Professional users need to understand how the manufacturer intends the device/equipment to be used, and how it works normally, to be able to use it effectively and safely.

Where relevant professional users should:

- be aware of differences between models, compatibility with other products
- be able to fit accessories
- be able to use any controls appropriately
- understand any displays, indicators, alarms, etc.
- cleaning and decontamination requirements
- demonstrate how to use the product
- understand the importance of reporting device-related adverse incidents to the MHRA.

End users

End users, i.e. service users or carers, need to understand the intended use and normal functioning of the device in order to use it effectively and safely.

Where relevant, training for end user should cover:

- limitations on use
- how to fit accessories
- how to use any controls appropriately
- understand displays, indicators, alarms, etc. and how to respond to them
- understand requirements for maintenance and decontamination; recognise when the device is not working properly and know what to do about it, e.g. troubleshoot
- understand the importance of reporting device-related adverse incidents to the MHRA.

Information, record management and manufacturer's instructions

It is crucial that all of the information relating to medical device management is co-ordinated, centrally controlled, and kept in a safe and accessible location. Good record keeping is essential for the safe management of medical devices. A significant amount of information relating specifically to equipment can be held electronically in the community equipment IT systems.

The ability to hold vast amounts of information electronically will play a crucial part when conducting planned maintenance schedules, or when carrying out a product recall. It is also most important to ensure information held against products is valid and up to date. This would be particularly important should an investigation take place following an untoward incident.

Some IT systems for managing community equipment are quite advanced and are capable of assisting with most aspects of medical device management. For example, they can hold manufacturers' information, which can be downloaded by professional and end users. They are also capable of sending out medical device alerts to professional users.

It is also important to ensure approved protocols are followed when deleting information. It may be necessary to have archive arrangements in place. This should be reflected in local policy.

As can be seen, careful consideration should be given to information management and record keeping, and should be clearly set out within the medical device management policy for the provision of community equipment.

Audit and review
Random internal quality audits and reviews will be carried out on all elements of maintenance and repair to ensure that the correct procedures are in place and that they are being adhered to.

Decontamination & disposal processes
Code standard 15 clearly sets out the decontamination responsibilities for community equipment providers. It is important that this is clearly set out within the medical device policy, with specific reference to community equipment.

Disposal of equipment is an area which does not generally receive much attention, but given the potential for associated cross contamination risks a safe disposal process is essential. Some issues which need to be factored in when considering this process include:

- The expected life cycle of a piece of equipment, i.e. should certain pieces of equipment be disposed after certain periods.

- Development of replacement criteria, e.g. whether the equipment is damaged or worn out beyond economic repair, poor reliability, clinical or technical obsolescence, changes in local policies for device use, absence of manufacturer/supplier support, non-availability of correct replacement parts, non-availability of specialist repair knowledge, users' opinions, possible benefits of new model (features, usability, more clinically effective, lower running costs), or the lifecycle of the medical device.

- Manufacturers should provide the best methods of waste disposal. They should be able to provide details of the current techniques and processes applicable to their products.

- Where applicable, equipment should be decontaminated before disposal, and supplied with a certificate of decontamination.

- When transporting equipment, arrangements will need to be in place to ensure that it is appropriately packaged and secured. 'The Carriage of Dangerous Goods by Road Regulations 1996' legislation applies to the safe transport of goods by road. It is of equal importance to ensure that consideration is given to disposal arrangements for third party contractors. It should also not be expected to subject professional users or end users to potentially illegal disposal practice, e.g. having to dispose contaminated equipment in cars, putting contaminated and soiled equipment in household bins.

- Decommissioning aims to make equipment safe and unusable, while minimising damage to the environment and to individuals. Any equipment deemed unfit for reuse should be decommissioned. Decommissioning should include decontamination, making safe, and making unusable. This is to ensure that an inappropriate person does not use the equipment and expose themselves to potential hazards.

The above points highlight the necessity for decontamination and disposal issues to be clearly documented in a community equipment medical device management policy.

Appendix 6

Health and Safety Executive (HSE) 'POPMAR' Model

The following summary of the POPMAR Model has been adapted from HSE's 'Successful Health and Safety Management' booklet[37].

Step 1: Policy setting

Health and safety policy should be developed to decide the selection of people, equipment and materials, the way work is done and how goods and services are provided. A written statement on the arrangements for implementing and monitoring policy shows that hazards have been identified and risks assessed, eliminated or controlled.

Step 2: Organise staff

To make the health and safety policy effective, staff should be involved and committed to making it work. This is often referred to as a 'positive health and safety culture', of which the following five 'C's are the essential aspects – as set out by HSE:

   i.   **Commitment** in being clear about your intent to achieve excellence in health and safety.
   ii. **Competence**: training and advice for all staff, using specialists where necessary.
   iii. **Control**: monitor staff knowledge and awareness.
   iv. **Co-operation**: involve staff in the reviewing of problems and procedures.
   v.   **Communication**: regular discussion on health and safety and easy access to information.

Step 3: Plan and set standards

Planning is the key to ensuring that health and safety works. It is advisable to record plans in writing. Planning should provide for:

---

[37] Health and Safety Executive (1997) *Successful Health and Safety Management*; HS(G)65; HSE Books.

- identification of hazards and risk assessment
- compliance with the health and safety laws that apply to your business
- consultation with staff, managers, and subcontractors
- standards set out how staff in your organisation deliver the policy and control risks. The standard must be 'measurable, achievable and realistic'.

Step 4: Measure performance

As in other areas, it is necessary to measure health and safety performance to judge success. There are two key components to effective monitoring:

i. **Active** monitoring (before things go wrong): regular inspection to ensure standards are being implemented and objectives are being met.
ii. **Reactive** monitoring (after things go wrong): investigating injuries, cases of illness, property damage and near misses - identifying why performance was substandard.

Priority should be given where risks are greatest and information referred to people with authority to take remedial action, such as organisational and policy changes.

Step 5: Audit and Review – learning from experience

Audits, by staff or external auditors, complement monitoring activities by looking to see if health and safety policy, organisation and systems are actually achieving the right results. They should be concerned with the reliability and effectiveness of health and safety policy and pay particular attention to:

- the degree of compliance with health and safety performance standards (including legislation)
- areas where standards are absent or inadequate
- achievement of stated objectives within given time-scales.

Appendix 7

Supporting guidance relating to the choice of decontamination method appropriate to the degree of infection risk associated with the intended use of the equipment. [38]

Classification of infection risk associated with the decontamination of medical devices

Risk	Application of item	Recommendation
High	In close contact with broken skin or broken mucous membrane. Introduced into sterile body areas.	Cleaning followed by sterilization.
Medium	In contact with mucous membranes. Contaminated with particularly virulent or readily transmissible organisms. Before use on immunocompromised patients.	Cleaning followed by sterilization or disinfection. NB: Where sterilization will damage equipment, cleaning followed by high level disinfection may be used as an alternative.
Low	In contact with healthy skin. Not in contact with patient.	Cleaning.

Other factors to consider when choosing a method of decontamination include the:
- nature of the contamination
- time required for processing
- heat, pressure, moisture and chemical tolerance of the item
- availability of the processing equipment
- quality and risks associated with the decontamination method.

---

[38] Taken from MHRA '*Managing Medical Devices*' document (MHRA DB2006 (05) November 2006). Accessible on MHRA website only.

Appendix 8

Glossary

assessment	evaluation of an individual's need by a person who is professionally qualified and approved to do so.
assistive technology	product, device or service designed to enable independence for disabled or older people.
carer	any person, paid or unpaid, who undertakes a caring role for a service user.
clinical services interface	aspects of clinical responsibilities that interface with community equipment services.
commissioner	individual within Local Authority, NHS, or other public service, appointed to be responsible for the strategic level process of planning, specifying, securing and monitoring services to meet people's needs.
complex, specialist and children's equipment	items of community equipment which are not generally classified as standard or routine equipment. Note. These items will typically be complex by design and may be bespoke or specially adapted or tailored to meet the particular needs of the individual for whom they are prescribed.
continuing healthcare equipment	equipment supplied to a person who has been accepted as having continuing healthcare needs.
cross border protocol	protocol used to provide guidance relating to the provision of community equipment across geographic boundaries or partnership borders.
direct payments	money given to service users to enable them to purchase equipment (or services) themselves.

disabled facilities grants	grants provided by Local Authorities to help meet the cost of adapting a property for the needs of a disabled person.
eligibility criteria	level of assessment of need to which an organisation will seek to provide services. Note. Local Authorities currently use four different levels of need: (i). critical; (ii). substantial; (iii). moderate; (iv). low.
minor adaptations	minor alterations made to a service user's property. Note. Minor Adaptations are for the purpose of increasing or maintaining functional independence to enable the service user to remain in their own home, to ensure safety and/or to assist carers by minimising the physical demands placed on them.
national service framework	systematic approach for improving healthcare standards and quality. Note. NSFs are implemented in partnership with social care and other organisations. They set national standards and define service models for a service or care group, and establish performance measures against which progress within agreed timescales will be measured.
partnership board	the structure for the management and planning of the provision of a community equipment service across a number of partner organisations in one geographical area.
prescriber	person permitted by one of the purchasing authorities to assess a service user's need for an adaptation or equipment, and to requisition the item from the equipment service.
provider	organisation or individual responsible for supplying the specified equipment services on behalf of the purchasing or commissioning authorities.

recycling	retrieval, cleaning and decontamination, maintenance, repair and refurbishment, so that equipment is fit for reissue.
requisition	formal order request for community equipment.
self-assessment	service user assessing their own needs and, where appropriate, selecting their own items of community equipment.
service user	person who requires and uses community equipment aids or adaptations supplied by the service following a needs assessment.
single assessment	assessment that ensures service users receive appropriate, effective and timely responses to their health and social care needs, and that professional resources are used effectively, by multi-agency working across all relevant disciplines.
social model of disability	model focusing on structures and their barriers which disabled individuals experience (for example, inaccessible transport, housing and education provision) and provides tools for dismantling and preventing these. Note. This contrasts with the medical model, which looks at medical impairments as the main reason for difficulties experienced by disabled people.
trusted assessor	staff such as assistants and support workers who have undergone specific training to assess people requiring disability equipment, usually in relation to 'straightforward' and low-risk needs.